ANY YEAR
DIARY

Written by

Carmel Carberry

www.gardenlandministries.org

INTRODUCTION AND COPYRIGHTS

This diary is suitable to use any week of any year. It begins with pages available to record personal details (pages 2-3) followed by a 'dates to remember' section (pages 4-5) and a yearly planner chart (pages 6-7)

The main diary section has weekly pages with spaces for the user to write in, alongside colour photographs and helpful Bible insights to bless and encourage. Pages for personal note making are also available at the back of the dairy.

'Notes of encouragement' from *Gardenland Ministries* (please see end pages for more info*)* can be found on pages 9-11 / 30-31 / 54-55 / 72-73 / 90-91 / 110-111

Bible verses throughout this book are personalized and paraphrased, but references are clearly stated for further reflection and study if the reader desires

Personal Notes / Details

....

....

....

....

....

....

....

....

....

....

....

....

....

God loves you dearly
(Taken from Jude 1)

Personal Notes / Details

....

....

....

....

....

....

....

....

....

....

....

....

....

you are secure in Jesus
(Taken from Jude 1)

Dates to Remember

	Birthdays / Special Occasions
Jan	
Feb	
Mar	
Apr	
May	
Jun	

Dates to Remember

	Birthdays / Special Occasions
Jul	
Aug	
Sept	
Oct	
Nov	
Dec	

JANUARY	FEBRUARY	MARCH	APRIL	MAY	JUNE
1	1	1	1	1	1
2	2	2	2	2	2
3	3	3	3	3	3
4	4	4	4	4	4
5	5	5	5	5	5
6	6	6	6	6	6
7	7	7	7	7	7
8	8	8	8	8	8
9	9	9	9	9	9
10	10	10	10	10	10
11	11	11	11	11	11
12	12	12	12	12	12
13	13	13	13	13	13
14	14	14	14	14	14
15	15	15	15	15	15
16	16	16	16	16	16
17	17	17	17	17	17
18	18	18	18	18	18
19	19	19	19	19	19
20	20	20	20	20	20
21	21	21	21	21	21
22	22	22	22	22	22
24	24	24	24	24	24
25	25	25	25	25	25
26	26	26	26	26	26
27	27	27	27	27	27
28	28	28	28	28	28
29	29	29	29	29	29
30		30	30	30	30
31		31		31	

JULY	AUGUST	SEPTEMBER	OCTOBER	NOVEMBER	DECEMBER
1	1	1	1	1	1
2	2	2	2	2	2
3	3	3	3	3	3
4	4	4	4	4	4
5	5	5	5	5	5
6	6	6	6	6	6
7	7	7	7	7	7
8	8	8	8	8	8
9	9	9	9	9	9
10	10	10	10	10	10
11	11	11	11	11	11
12	12	12	12	12	12
13	13	13	13	13	13
14	14	14	14	14	14
15	15	15	15	15	15
16	16	16	16	16	16
17	17	17	17	17	17
18	18	18	18	18	18
19	19	19	19	19	19
20	20	20	20	20	20
21	21	21	21	21	21
22	22	22	22	22	22
24	24	24	24	24	24
25	25	25	25	25	25
26	26	26	26	26	26
27	27	27	27	27	27
28	28	28	28	28	28
29	29	29	29	29	29
30	30	30	30	30	30
31	31		31		31

you hold a special

place in Gods heart

A Word of Love from The Heart of God....His Son

I AM the way, and the truth, and the life. Come to the Father through The Son. I came to show you what the Father is really like, for I came from the very heart of God to call you to be His child forever.

No darkness can ever extinguish My Light, for it is eternal and ever-living. As God's very own child, My Light lives in you.

So let your light shine for all to see, which honours your Father in Heaven, who loves you all the time, yesterday, today and forever!

I AM The Bridge of eternal life, I do not condemn, I offer forgiveness and love. Trust in Me with all your heart, and I will show you the way.

Related Bible References:
John 14:6 / John 1:12-18 / John 1:5 / Matt 5:16 / Col 1:27
Heb 13:8 / 1 John 3:1 / John 3:16-17 / Matt 11:28 / Prov 3:5-6

More articles, 'Teaching Letters' and 'Bible Studies' are available to view and download on our website and also at: www.facebook.com/groups/gardenlandministries
If you would like to receive these by e-mail, please contact: gardenlandministries@gmail.com

When you give yourself to Christ
you become a new creation

See 2 Corinthians 5:17-21

This is who you are because of Jesus and all He has done for you. So, with a heart of faith you can declare.....

I am chosen (Eph 1:4) loved (Jer 31:3) and precious (Is 43:4)

I am valuable (Luke12:7) for I am the 'apple of His eye' (Zech 2:8)

My name is engraved on His hand (Is 49:15-16)

I am fearfully and wonderfully made (Ps 139:14)

I am gifted (1 Cor 1:7) ~ I am saved by grace (2 Tim1:9)

God has a good plan for me (Jer 29:11)

I am never alone because He is always with me (Heb 13:5)

Nothing can separate me from Him (Rom 8:38)

No one can snatch me out of His hand (John 10:28)

He will never drive me away (John 6:37)

God Himself sings over me! (Zeph 3:17)

I am able to do all things through Him (Phil 4:13)

I am able to do good works (Eph 2:10)

I am able to bear good fruit (John 15:16)

I am being transformed into His likeness (2 Cor 3:18)

I am a member of God's family (Heb 2:11)

Proverbs 3:5-6 encourages you to
trust in God with your whole heart
and He will guide your path

MONDAY		
TUESDAY		
WEDNESDAY		
THURSDAY		
FRIDAY		
SATURDAY		
SUNDAY		

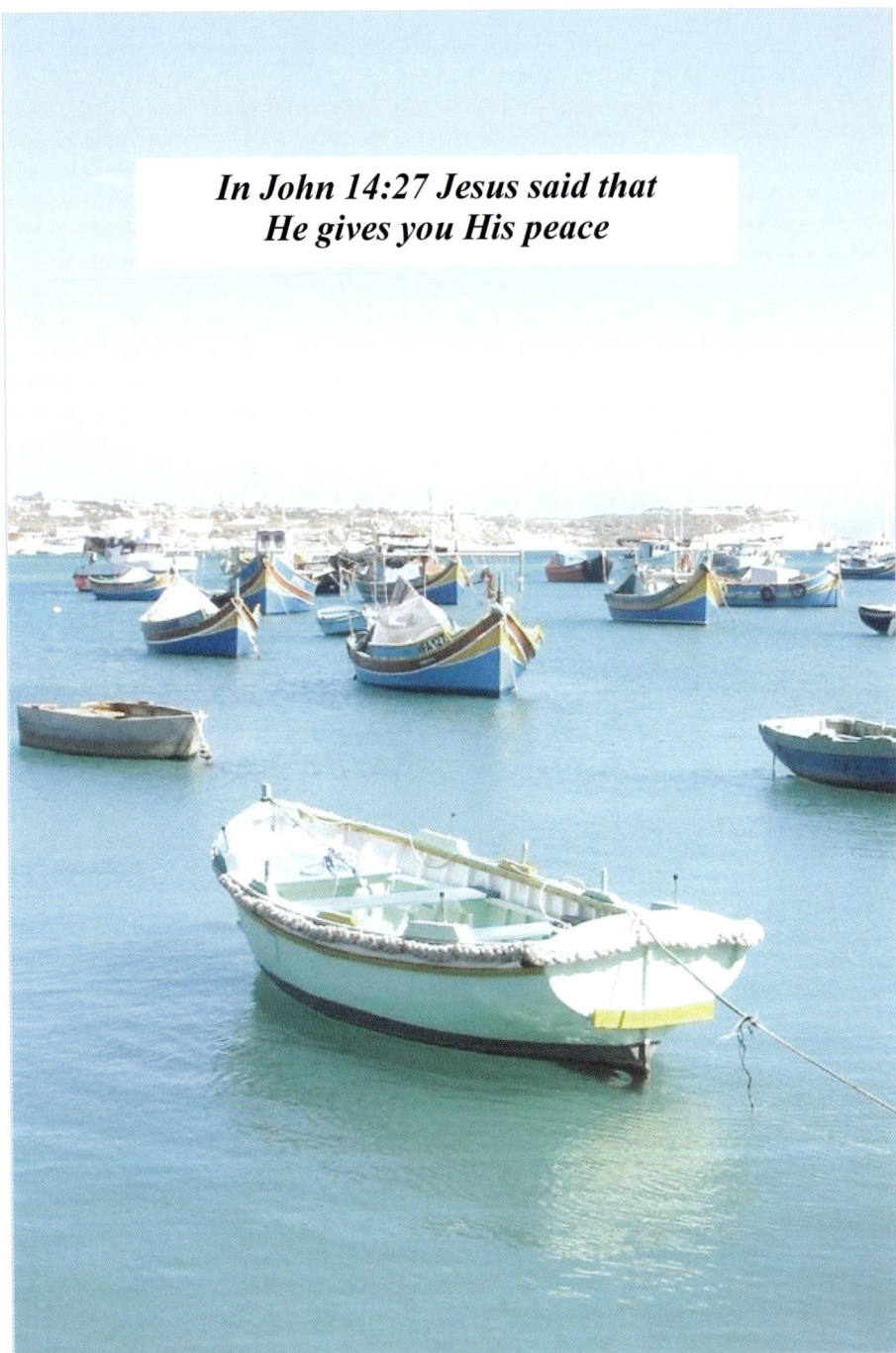

In John 14:27 Jesus said that
He gives you His peace

MONDAY		
TUESDAY		
WEDNESDAY		
THURSDAY		
FRIDAY		
SATURDAY		
SUNDAY		

Nehemiah 8:10 says that you can find strength in the joy of God

MONDAY		Date
TUESDAY		Date
WEDNESDAY		Date
THURSDAY		Date
FRIDAY		Date
SATURDAY		Date
SUNDAY		Date

Matthew 10:29-31 tells us that
God even cares for sparrows,
therefore trust that He cares for you

MONDAY		Date
TUESDAY		Date
WEDNESDAY		Date
THURSDAY		Date
FRIDAY		Date
SATURDAY		Date
SUNDAY		Date

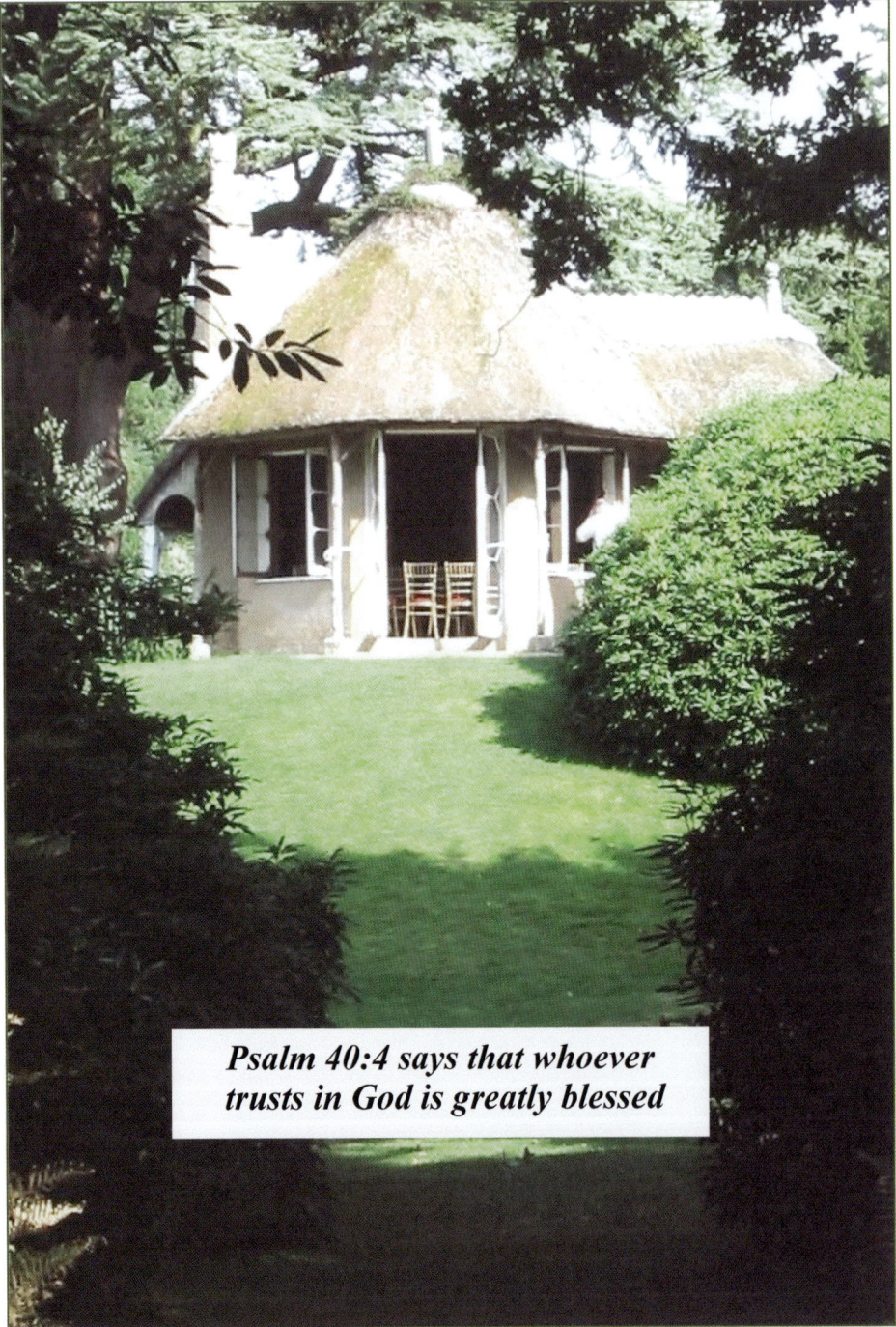

Psalm 40:4 says that whoever trusts in God is greatly blessed

MONDAY		Date
TUESDAY		Date
WEDNESDAY		Date
THURSDAY		Date
FRIDAY		Date
SATURDAY		Date
SUNDAY		Date

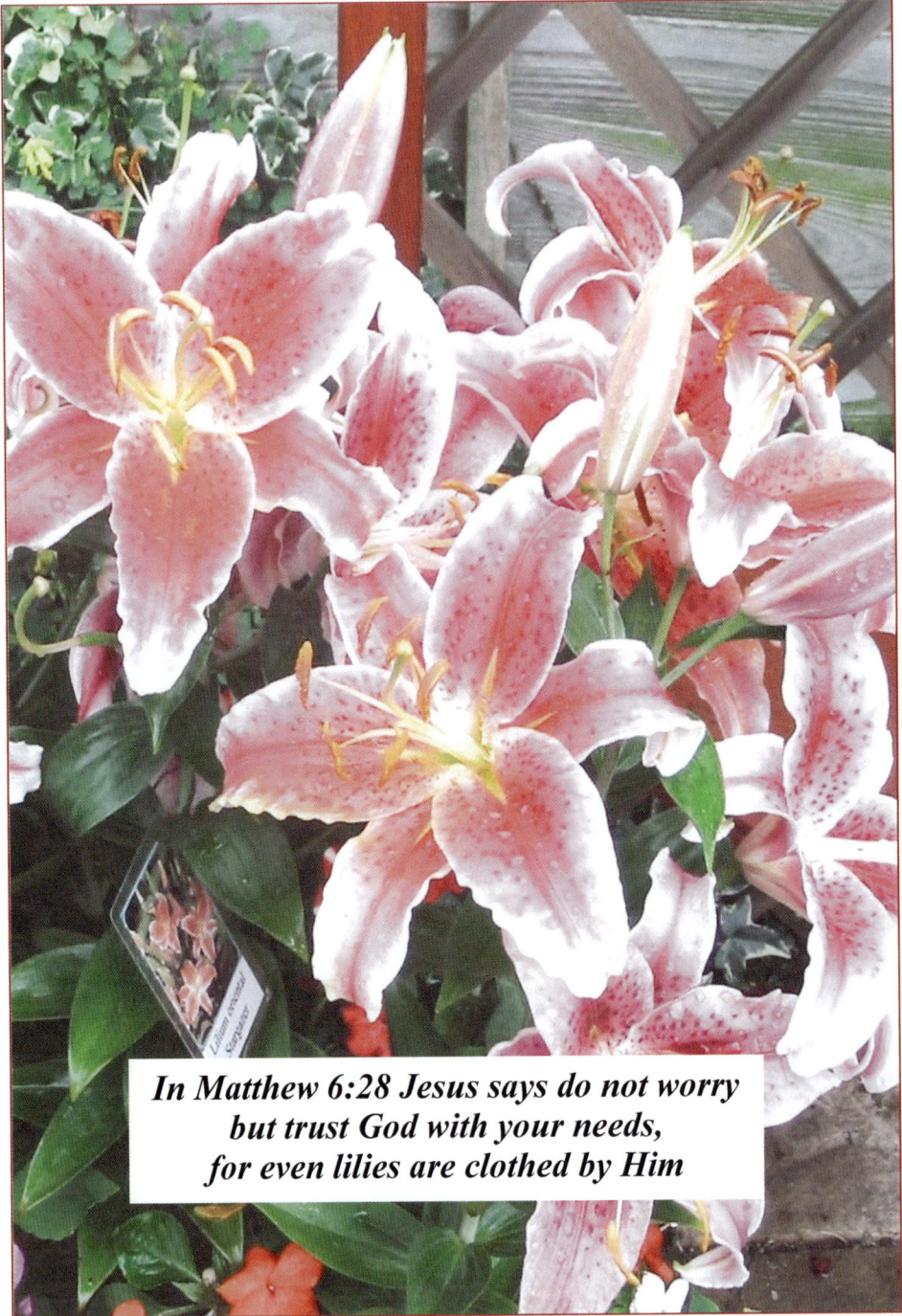

In Matthew 6:28 Jesus says do not worry
but trust God with your needs,
for even lilies are clothed by Him

MONDAY		Date
TUESDAY		Date
WEDNESDAY		Date
THURSDAY		Date
FRIDAY		Date
SATURDAY		Date
SUNDAY		Date

Psalm 18:2 says The Lord is a like a secure
'Rock' and that He is your salvation

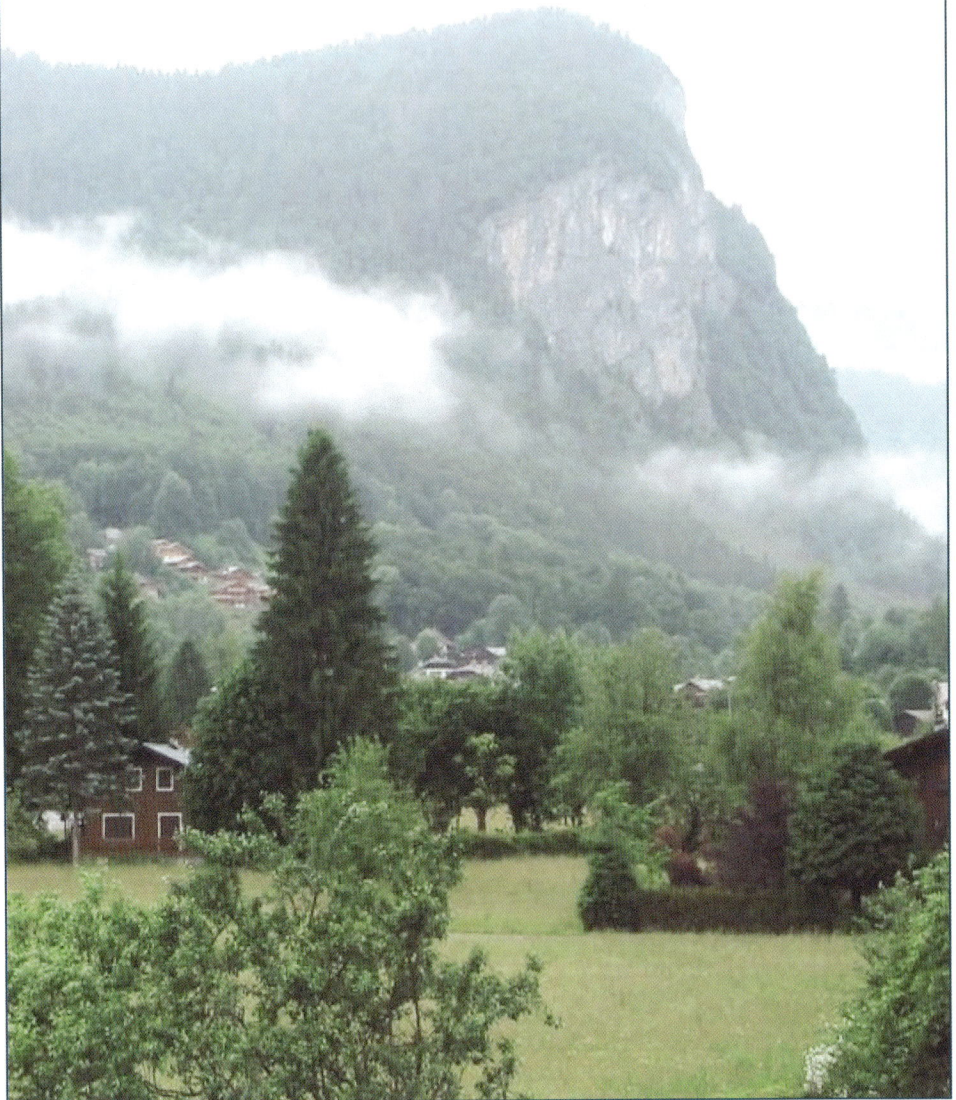

MONDAY		
TUESDAY		
WEDNESDAY		
THURSDAY		
FRIDAY		
SATURDAY		
SUNDAY		

Psalm 145:13 tells us that God is faithful

And that He is loving to all that He has made

MONDAY		
TUESDAY		
WEDNESDAY		
THURSDAY		
FRIDAY		
SATURDAY		
SUNDAY		

Habakkuk 2:14 tells us that one day the truth about His great love will be known across the earth, like the waters cover the sea

MONDAY		Date
TUESDAY		Date
WEDNESDAY		Date
THURSDAY		Date
FRIDAY		Date
SATURDAY		Date
SUNDAY		Date

The Bible tells us that all who believe and receive Jesus become children of God (*John 1:12*). The term 'sonship' is often used to express the position of being 'sons' which is an amazing truth to consider *(Rom 8:15)*

The New Testament letters clearly reveal that it is by faith in Christ alone that we are God's children. Thus, our position of 'sonship' is based solely on Him and all He has done for us, no matter what gender we are, or what background or nation we are from. It is all a gift of His wonderful grace (*Gal 3:26-29 / Eph 1:5*)

We are also shown that any troubles we may experience here and now are nothing compared with the 'glory to be revealed' in us and to us through being His kids! (*Rom 8:14-19*).

As His children, we need to be led by His Spirit daily in our lives and we need to remind ourselves that The Father Himself loves you and I so very much! (*1 John 3:1 / John 16:27*)

God knows His children and through our relationship with Him we can enjoy the freedom of knowing God as He truly is. We can live even here and now with a newness of life that is filled with Jesus (*Rom 6:4 / Rom 8:14*).

As we learn to follow His example through the truth of His Word and the leading of His Spirit, we begin to display His likeness in our lives. Although you and I remain individuals, distinct from each other, we also 'share the family likeness' as each child of God looks to his/her Heavenly Father! (*Rom 8:28-30*)

The character of Jesus is beautifully shown in *Gal 5:22-23*, where the fruit of The Spirit is listed for us: LOVE, PEACE, JOY, PATIENCE, KINDNESS, GOODNESS, FAITHFULNESS, GENTLENESS and SELF-CONTROL.

These traits, despite our own personal human imperfections, will still come to the fore in our lives as we look into the face of Jesus and reflect His nature back into the world around us (*2 Cor 3:18*)

This happens because you ARE a child of God, living your life in The Son (*Gal 2:20*). Consider a tree which bears fruit ~ it does so because it is a fruit bearing tree! Part of our 'sonship' is that we possess all of the wonderful spiritual fruit of Gal 5:22-23 as part of our eternal spirit, because of our union with Christ (*Gal 3:27*).

Therefore, using the analogy of the tree, as you and I put our 'spiritual roots' deep into the 'soil of God's eternal love and acceptance' (*Col 2:6-7*), keeping our hearts and minds on Him (*Is 26:3*), then we can't help but display this wonderful fruit at every 'harvestime of our lives' by His power at work in us as His sons and daughters (*Eph 1:19*)

The 'harvestime' could be any situation that we come across during which time we *depend on Him* ~ then the fruit will begin to make its presence known (*John 15:5*). Dependency on Jesus is acted out by our faith in Him. His grace is given freely to you and I, our act of faith is a response to His love (*Rom 3:24*)

The devotion of our hearts is not something we give because we HAVE to but because we WANT to. Our love and devotion to Jesus is a response to GOD'S DEVOTION TO US, because He has loved us first (*1 John 4:19*) and He has displayed His love perfectly through the gift of His Son (*John 3:16-17*)

Therefore ~ trust, hope and believe ~ and enjoy your sonship in The Son of God who loves you completely with everything He has! (*John 3:35/Jude 1*).

Prayer:
Thank You Father that I am your son! Thank You for loving me, for accepting me.
You have cleansed me from all sin for all time through all Jesus has done; therefore
I put my faith in Him, and rest my heart on His love. In Him my soul can enjoy
peace as You guide and lead me each day by Your Holy Spirit. For I am
a child of The Living God, holy and dearly loved, all because of Jesus!
Thank You Abba Father ~ my Daddy! Amen.

More articles, 'Teaching Letters' and 'Bible Studies' are available to view and download
on our website and also at: www.facebook.com/groups/gardenlandministries
If you would like to receive these by e-mail, please contact: gardenlandministries@gmail.com

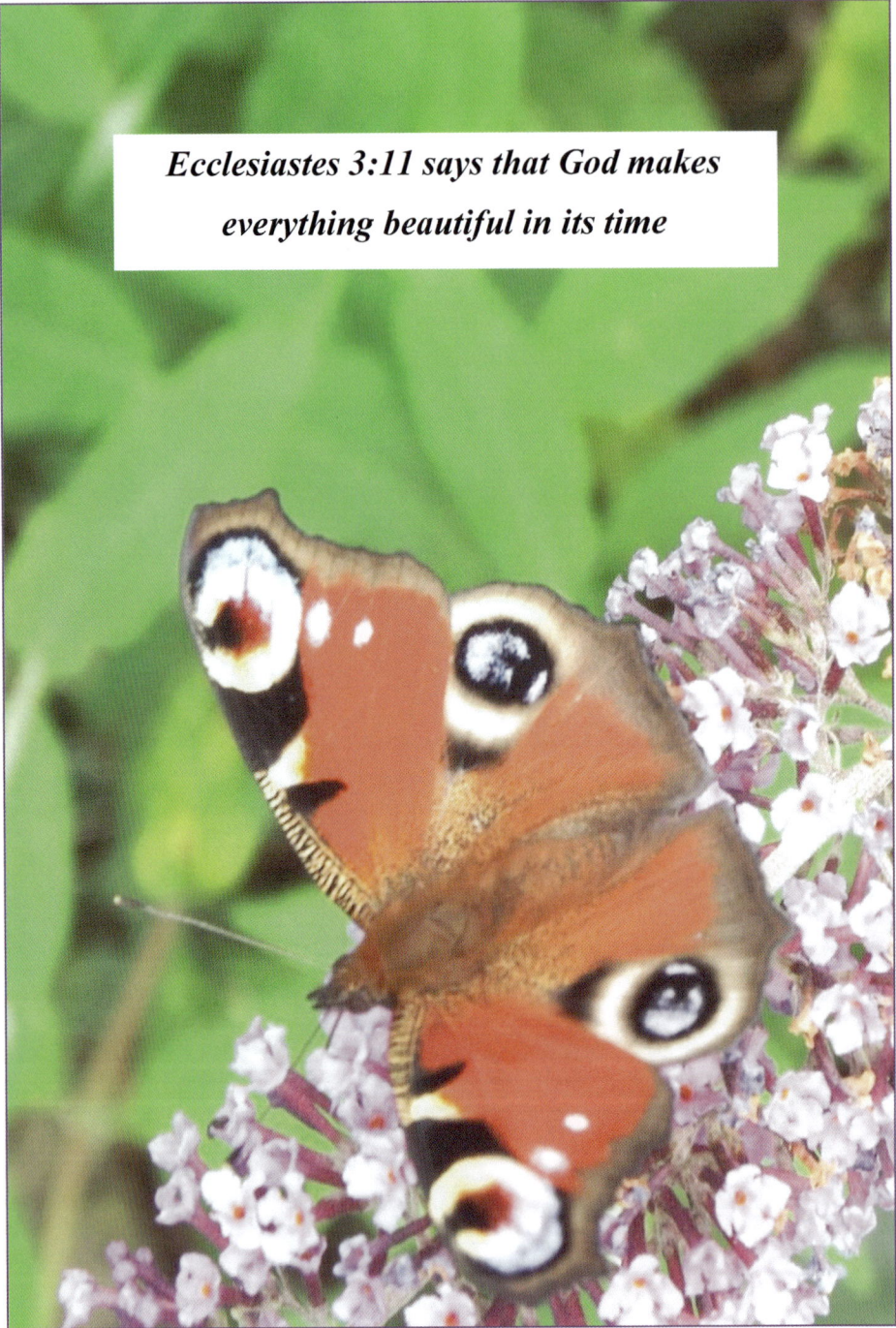

Ecclesiastes 3:11 says that God makes everything beautiful in its time

MONDAY		Date
TUESDAY		Date
WEDNESDAY		Date
THURSDAY		Date
FRIDAY		Date
SATURDAY		Date
SUNDAY		Date

In Mark 10:27 Jesus said that with God all things are possible

MONDAY		Date
TUESDAY		Date
WEDNESDAY		Date
THURSDAY		Date
FRIDAY		Date
SATURDAY		Date
SUNDAY		Date

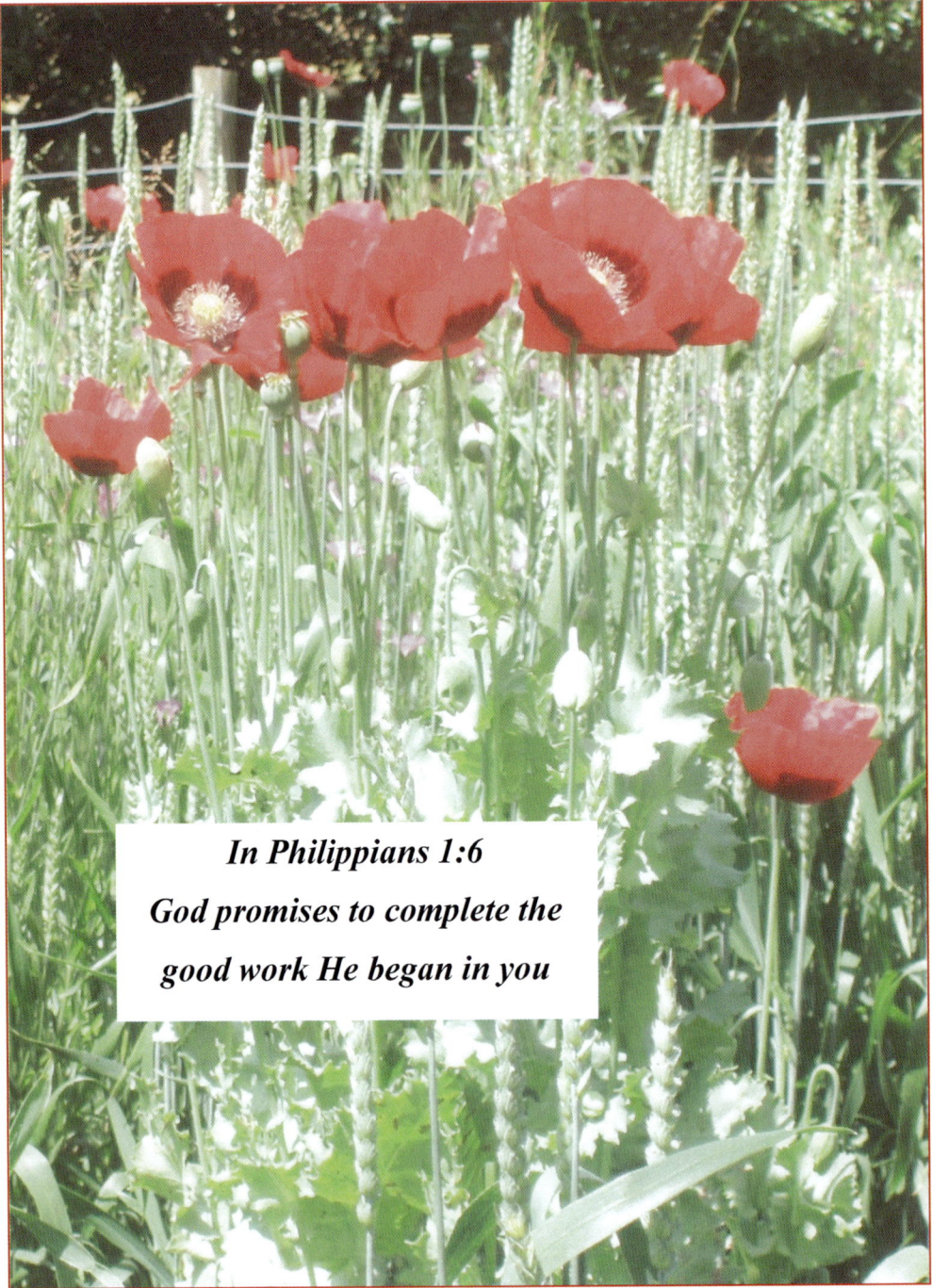

In Philippians 1:6
God promises to complete the
good work He began in you

MONDAY		Date
TUESDAY		Date
WEDNESDAY		Date
THURSDAY		Date
FRIDAY		Date
SATURDAY		Date
SUNDAY		Date

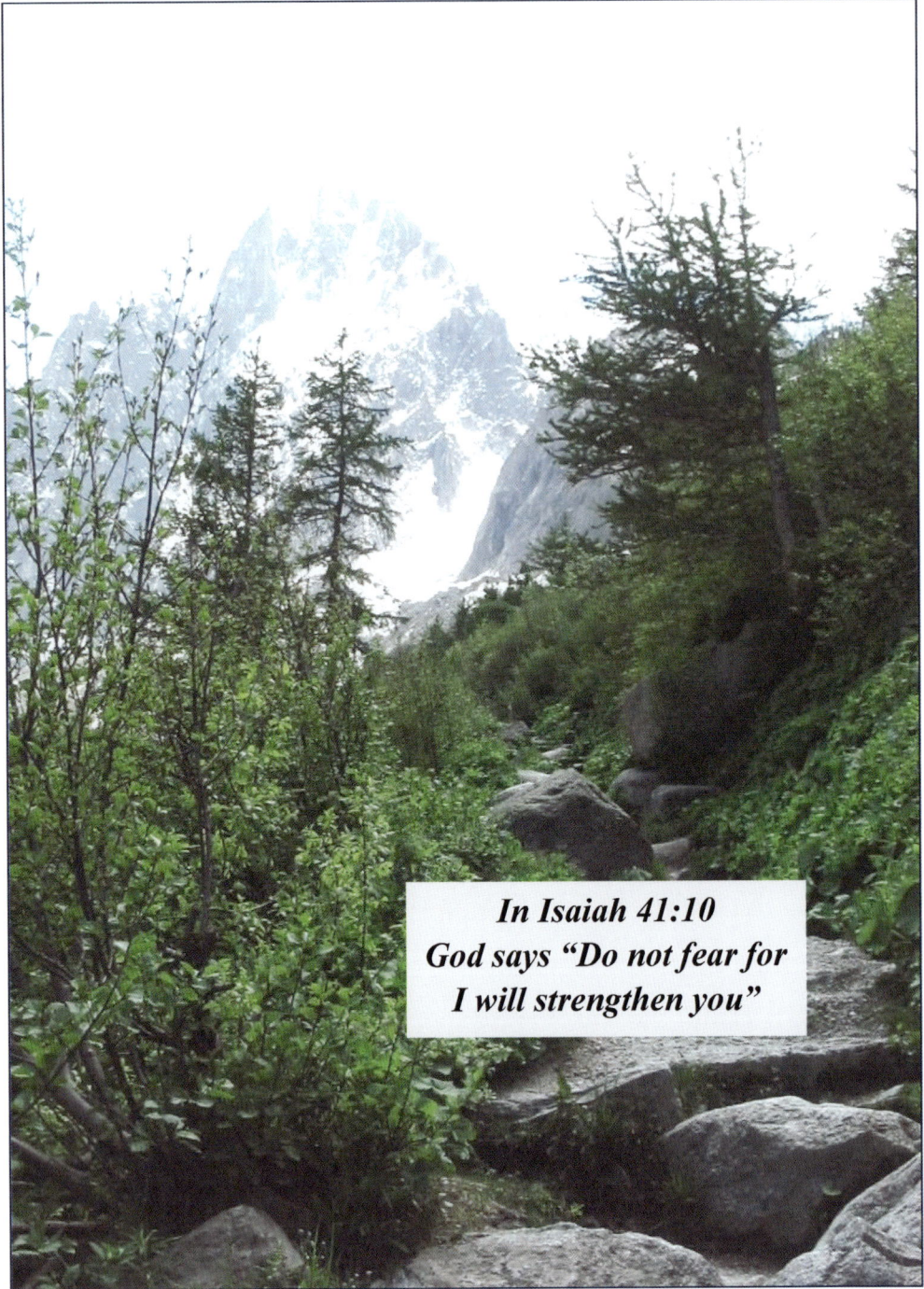

In Isaiah 41:10
God says "Do not fear for
I will strengthen you"

MONDAY		
TUESDAY		
WEDNESDAY		
THURSDAY		
FRIDAY		
SATURDAY		
SUNDAY		

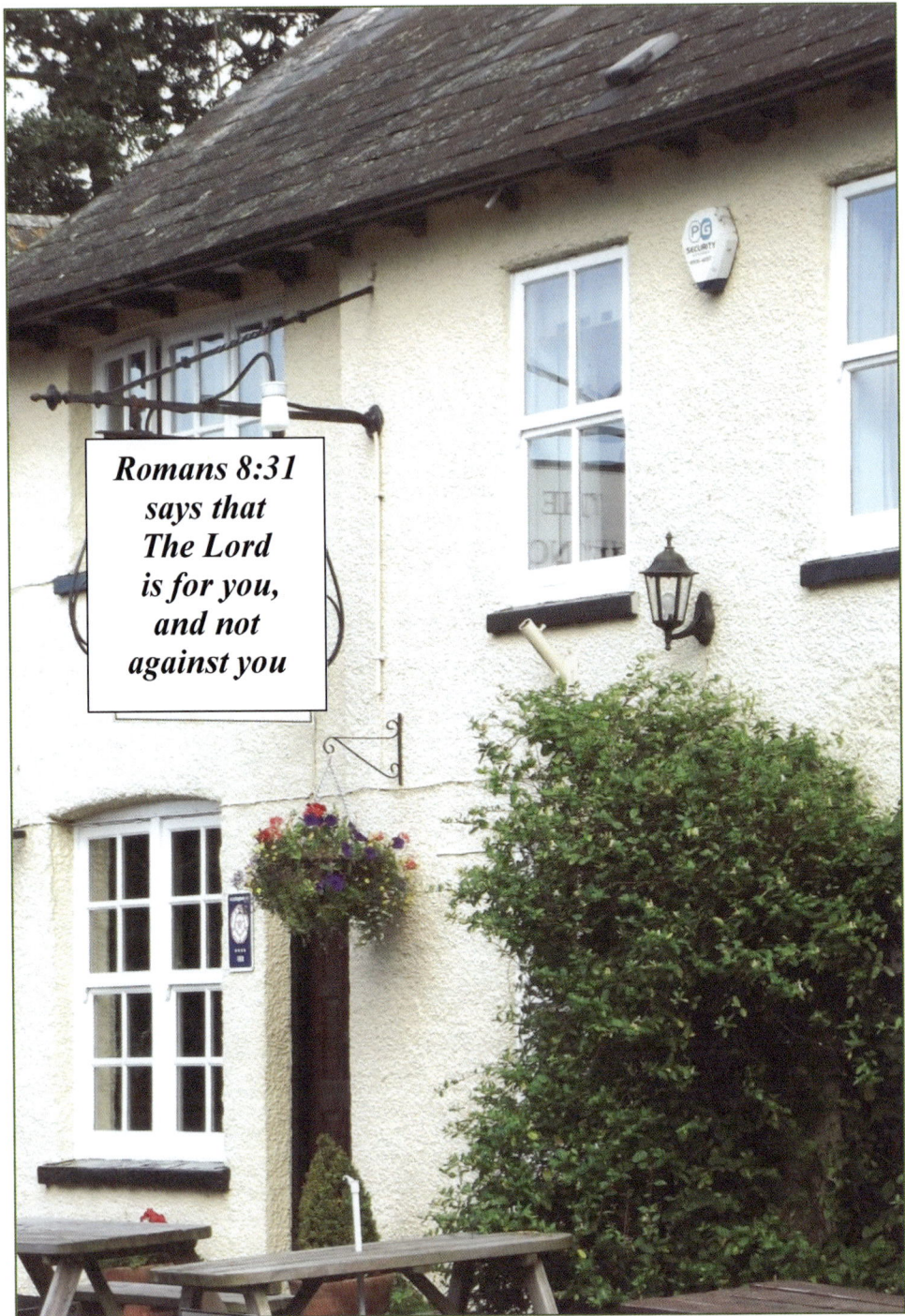

Romans 8:31
says that
The Lord
is for you,
and not
against you

MONDAY		Date
TUESDAY		Date
WEDNESDAY		Date
THURSDAY		Date
FRIDAY		Date
SATURDAY		Date
SUNDAY		Date

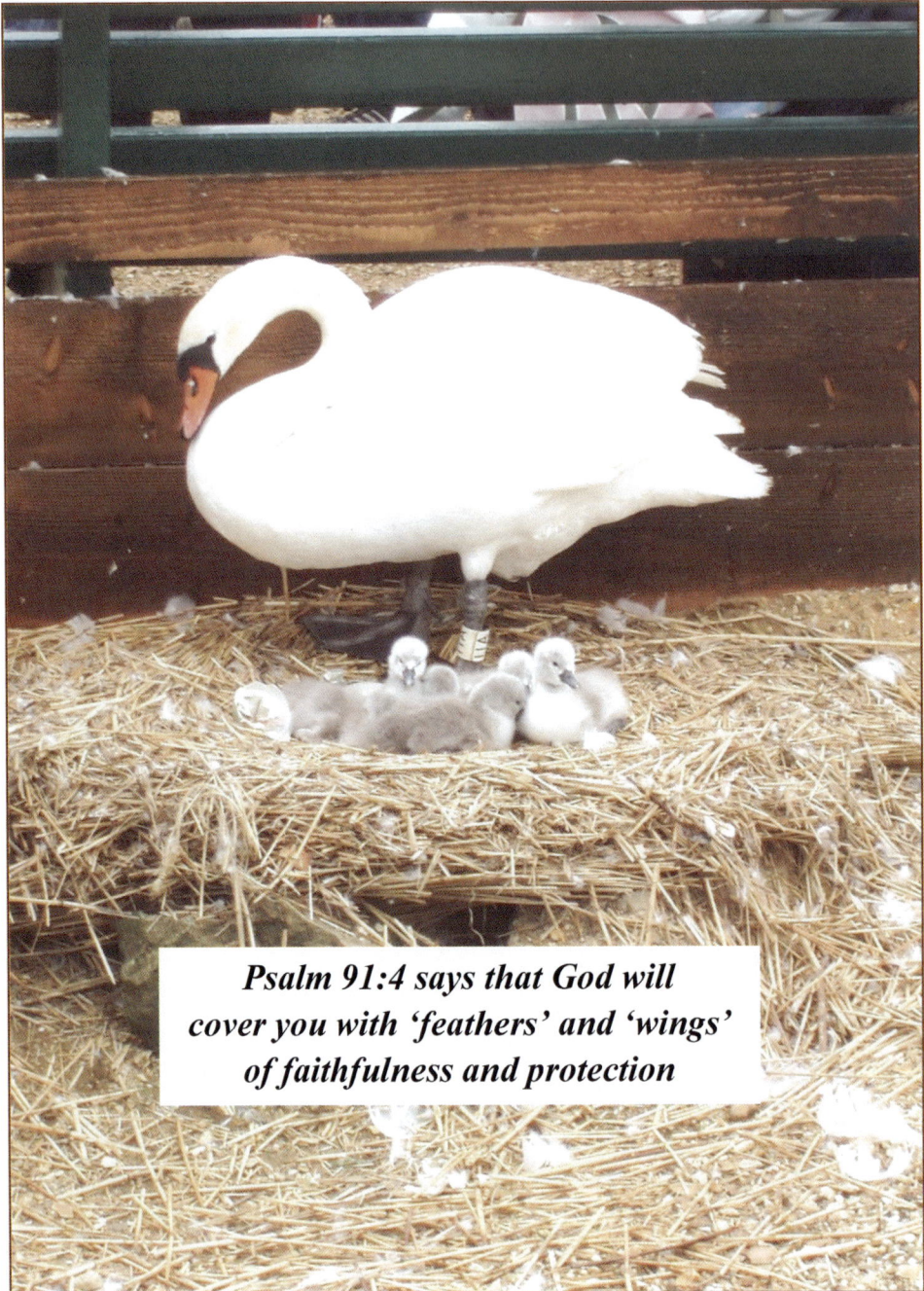

Psalm 91:4 says that God will cover you with 'feathers' and 'wings' of faithfulness and protection

MONDAY		Date
TUESDAY		Date
WEDNESDAY		Date
THURSDAY		Date
FRIDAY		Date
SATURDAY		Date
SUNDAY		Date

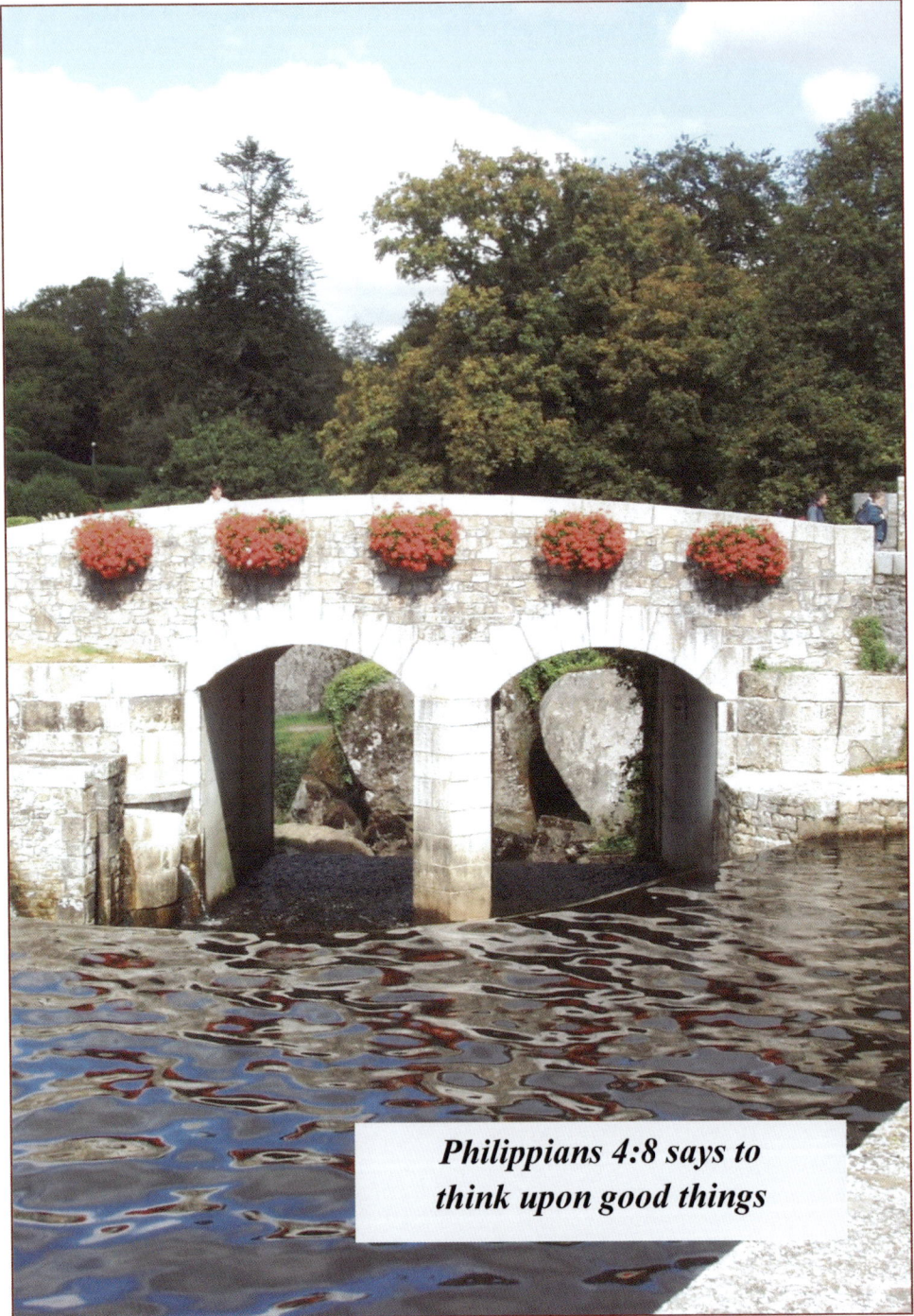

Philippians 4:8 says to think upon good things

MONDAY		Date
TUESDAY		Date
WEDNESDAY		Date
THURSDAY		Date
FRIDAY		Date
SATURDAY		Date
SUNDAY		Date

Ephesians 2:10 says that you
are God's work of art!

MONDAY		Date
TUESDAY		Date
WEDNESDAY		Date
THURSDAY		Date
FRIDAY		Date
SATURDAY		Date
SUNDAY		Date

*Psalm 118:29 encourages you to give thanks
to God, for He loves you always*

MONDAY		Date
TUESDAY		Date
WEDNESDAY		Date
THURSDAY		Date
FRIDAY		Date
SATURDAY		Date
SUNDAY		Date

Psalm 61:3 says that The Lord is a tower of strength ~ a place where you can find refuge and peace

MONDAY		Date
TUESDAY		Date
WEDNESDAY		Date
THURSDAY		Date
FRIDAY		Date
SATURDAY		Date
SUNDAY		Date

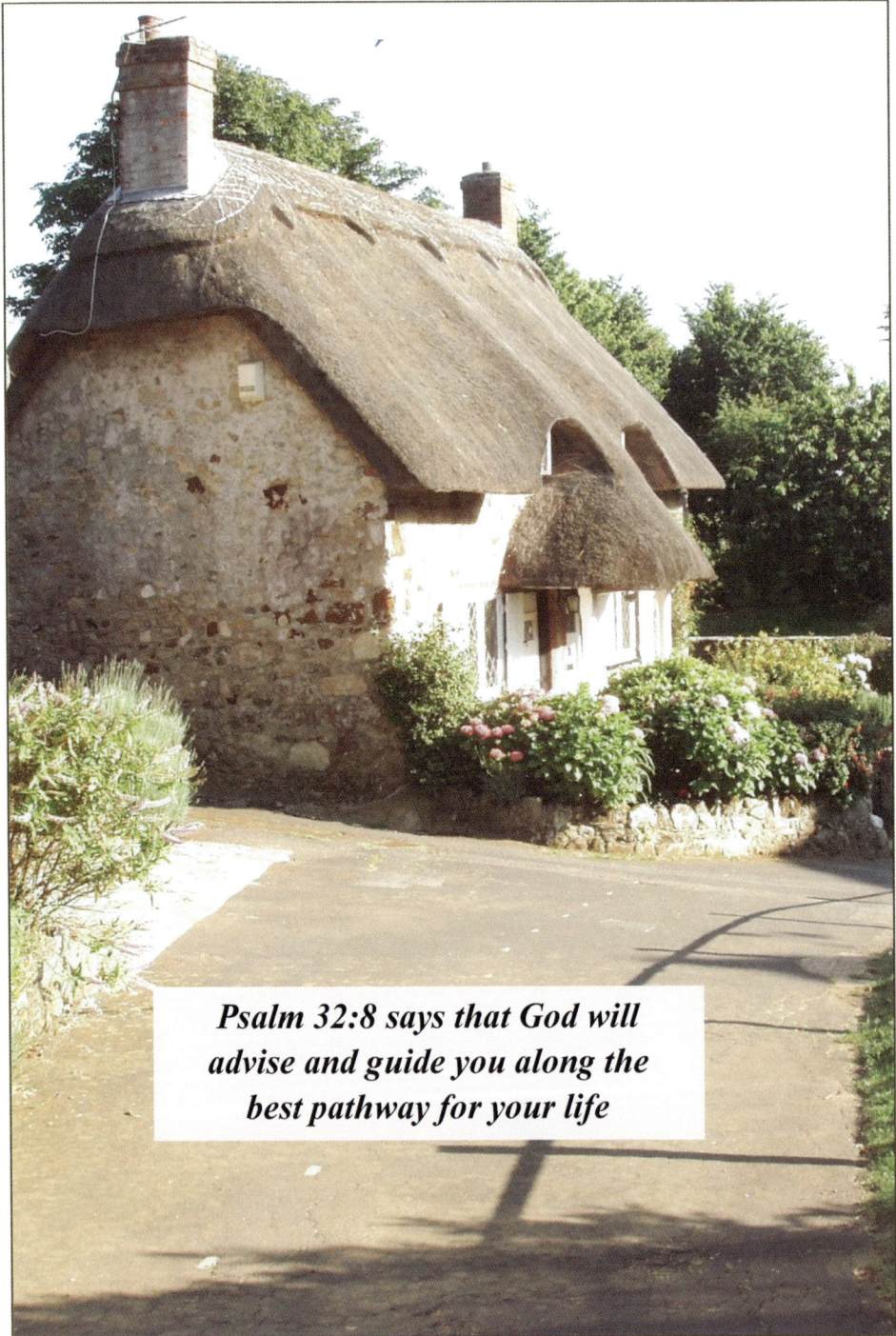

Psalm 32:8 says that God will advise and guide you along the best pathway for your life

MONDAY		
TUESDAY		
WEDNESDAY		
THURSDAY		
FRIDAY		
SATURDAY		
SUNDAY		

Notes of encouragement (3)

When you look in a mirror, what do you see? Is it merely your physical frame or do you see a 'new creation' with Christ living in you? All who put their faith in Jesus have an eternal hope and a life filled with purpose. Our real need is to be able to recognize our identity in Him. In Christ you can boldly say personally.....

I am justified and declared 'not guilty' in God's sight (Rom 3:24)

I am holy and acceptable to Him (1 Cor 1:2)

I have been given the righteousness of God (2 Cor 5:21)

All my sin is removed, and I am forgiven (Eph 1:7)

I can come to God with confidence (Eph 3:12)

I am blessed with all spiritual blessings (Eph 1:3)

I belong to God and am sealed by the Holy Spirit (Eph 1:13)

I am close to God and wrapped in His love (Eph 2:13 / Eph 1:4-5)

I am His workmanship and have a unique purpose (Eph 2:10)

I have a new nature, empowered by God's Spirit (Eph 4:23-24 / Col 3:10)

I am a child of The Living God (Gal 3:26)

He will never leave me nor reject me (Heb 13:5)

God does not condemn me (Rom 8:1)

I have eternal life within (John 6:47)

I am seated with Christ in Heavenly realms (Eph 2:6)

I belong to The Body of Christ (Rom 12:4-5)

I am a friend of God (John 15:15)

I have peace with God (Rom 5:1)

Nothing can separate me from His love (Rom 8:39)

I am complete in Him (Col 2:10)

The Father Himself loves me (John 16:27)

I have God's mercy and grace to help me in all situations (Heb 4:16)

Jesus Himself lives in me (Col 1:27)

I have His light within me (Eph 5:8-9)

His Holy Spirit lives in me (2 Cor 1:22)

My prayers are powerful and effective (James 5:16-18)

I have Christ's authority living within me (Luke 10:19)

The same power that raised Jesus from the dead lives in me (Eph 1:19-20)

I have power to overcome every obstacle in my life (1 John 5:4-5)

God loves me and holds me securely (Jude 1)

I have true fellowship with God Himself (1 John 5:20)

I am not under religious law, I am under God's grace (Rom 6:14)

I am created for good works, which God enables me to do (Eph 2:10 / Hab 3:19)

King Jesus is praying for me! (Heb 7:25)

Truth has set me free! (John 8:32)

I am strong in God and His mighty power (Eph 6:10)

I belong to a royal priesthood that shines out God's light (1 Peter 2:9)

God upholds me with His strength and power (Ps 20:6)

Christ is my strength in all things (Phil 4:13)

God gives me boldness in Him (2 Tim 1:7)

I live by faith in Jesus, who loves me (Gal 2:20)

God gives me a new song to sing (Ps 98:1)

In Christ, I always have hope (1 Thess 5:8)

Prayer:
Thank You Lord for these wonderful truths that show my true identity in Jesus.
Thank You for Your power that is at work in me. For I am a new creation made in
Your image, created to do good works that You enable me to do. I am not alone in this
world, for You are with me. Thank You that I am secure in Jesus, my Rock and my
Redeemer. I declare that You are my confidence, my hope and my joy; for
You give me a new song to sing and Your light to shine, the light of
Your eternal love. I praise and honour Your Name. Amen.

More articles, 'Teaching Letters' and 'Bible Studies' are available to view and download
on our website and also at: www.facebook.com/groups/gardenlandministries
If you would like to receive these by e-mail, please contact: gardenlandministries@gmail.com

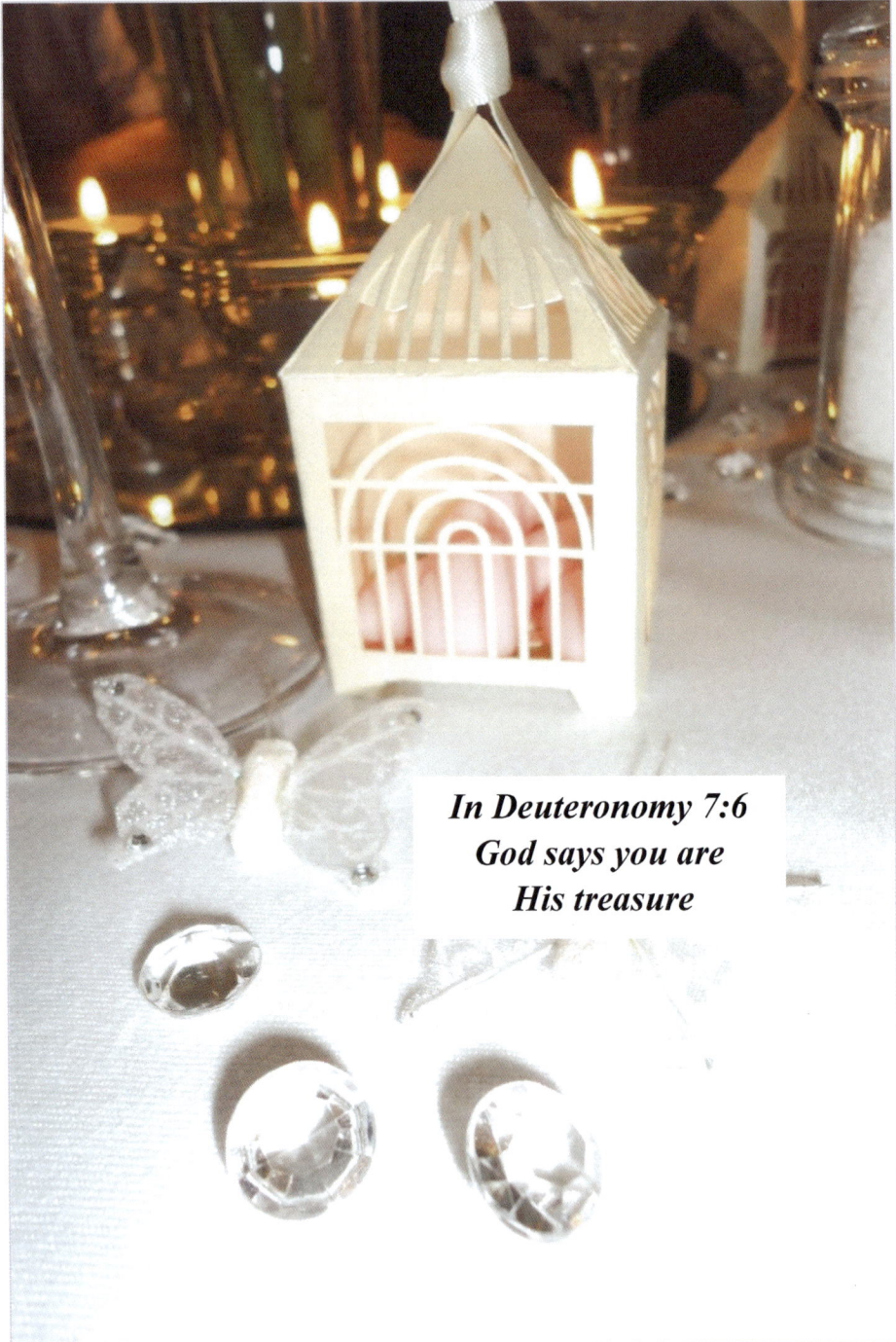

In Deuteronomy 7:6
God says you are
His treasure

MONDAY		Date
TUESDAY		Date
WEDNESDAY		Date
THURSDAY		Date
FRIDAY		Date
SATURDAY		Date
SUNDAY		Date

In John 4:14 Jesus says that He gives you the water of eternal life

MONDAY		Date
TUESDAY		Date
WEDNESDAY		Date
THURSDAY		Date
FRIDAY		Date
SATURDAY		Date
SUNDAY		Date

Jeremiah 31:3 says that God loves you with an everlasting love

MONDAY		
TUESDAY		
WEDNESDAY		
THURSDAY		
FRIDAY		
SATURDAY		
SUNDAY		

Psalm 100:3 calls God's people the 'Sheep of His Pasture'

MONDAY		
TUESDAY		
WEDNESDAY		
THURSDAY		
FRIDAY		
SATURDAY		
SUNDAY		

Luke 1:78 says that God has sent
His love to shine on you

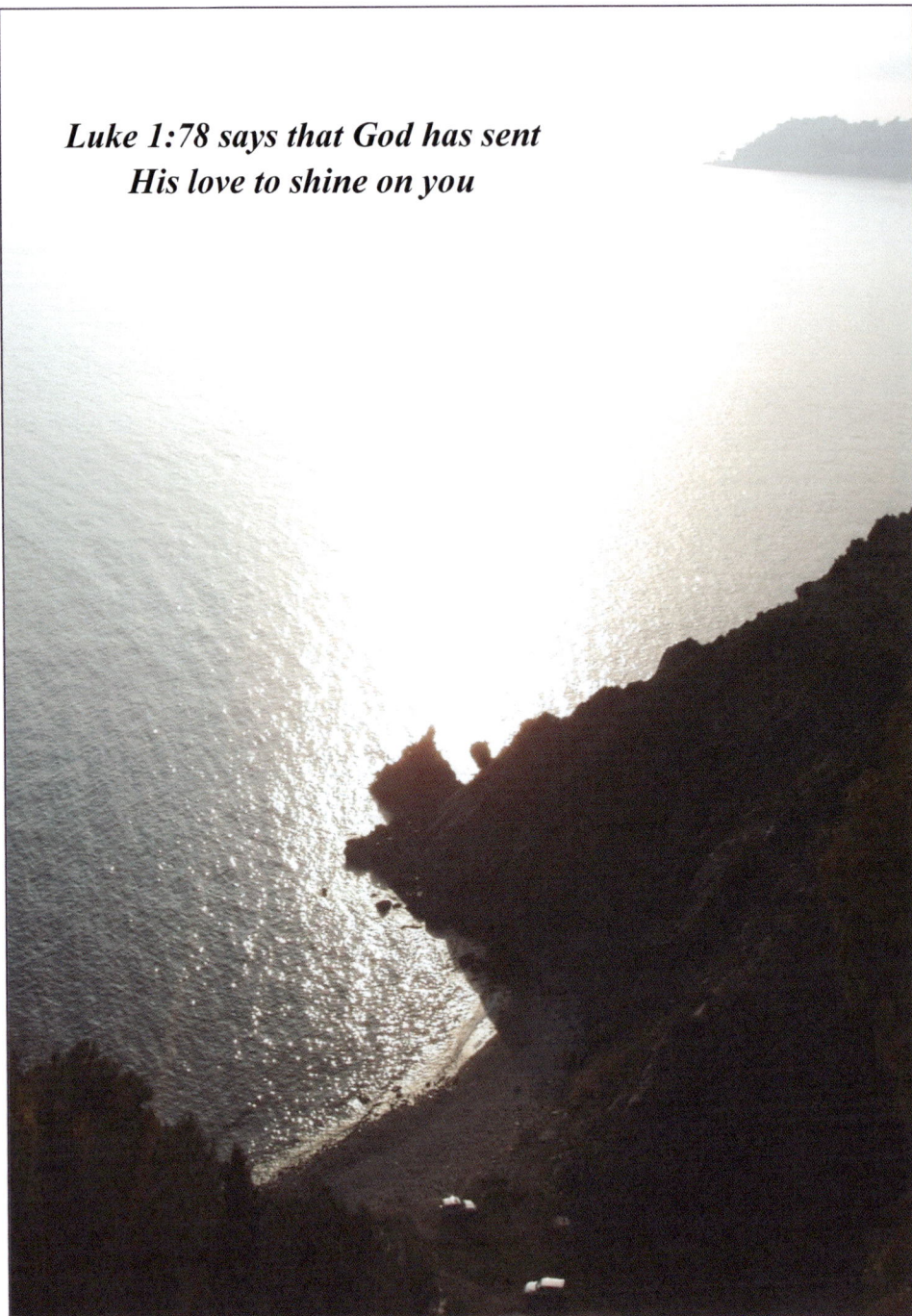

MONDAY		
TUESDAY		
WEDNESDAY		
THURSDAY		
FRIDAY		
SATURDAY		
SUNDAY		

Romans 8:39
says that NOTHING
can ever separate you
from God's love

MONDAY		Date
TUESDAY		Date
WEDNESDAY		Date
THURSDAY		Date
FRIDAY		Date
SATURDAY		Date
SUNDAY		Date

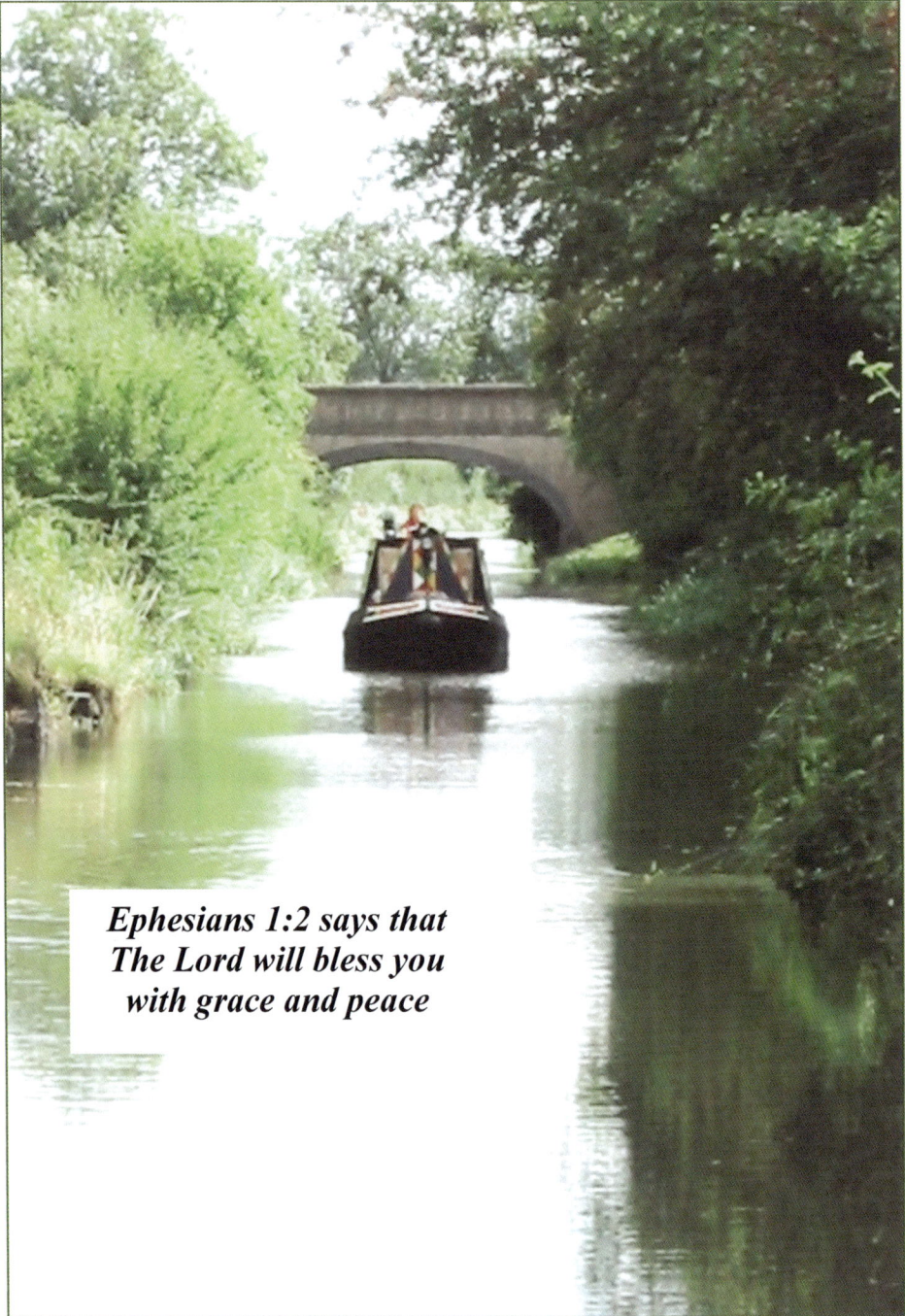

Ephesians 1:2 says that
The Lord will bless you
with grace and peace

MONDAY		Date
TUESDAY		Date
WEDNESDAY		Date
THURSDAY		Date
FRIDAY		Date
SATURDAY		Date
SUNDAY		Date

*Isaiah 40:31 says that
God will renew your
strength like the eagle*

MONDAY		
TUESDAY		
WEDNESDAY		
THURSDAY		
FRIDAY		
SATURDAY		
SUNDAY		

Relationships involve communication ~ when we talk to each other, we have the opportunity to share our inner most feelings, thoughts and desires with one-another. That interaction can prompt a strong bond between people, a bond of trust and appreciation, a bond of friendship, love and commitment.

In the same way, when we talk with God we can learn more about Him and share our inner most feelings, thoughts and desires with Him. And the amazing thing is, that He wants to share His heart with you and I too.

Prayer is communication with God. It helps develop our relationship with Him, which is what Christianity is all about – not just knowing about God but *knowing Him personally.* Jesus taught His disciples a pattern (or model) to follow when praying (*Matt 6:5-13*). Jesus said, "*when* you pray", rather than "*if* you pray", which suggests He considered it to be the natural thing to do.

Our prayers are not in vain, they are reaching Someone who deeply cares about us…. Someone who is alive and well and listening to us (*1 Peter 3:12+18*). God always answers our prayers,

BUT sometimes His answer *may not* be what we expect. It could even be 'no' or 'not yet'. If God had given me everything I had ever asked for or wanted (since my natural mind can change frequently!) I would probably be in quite a mess.

But God knows my heart and He also knows what is best, for my present and future, and for those I love around me which my decisions and choices can affect. Of course it can be very difficult if we *have* prayed for ourselves, or a loved one, over a problem and *not* seen the answer we would have liked to have done.

Yet, as we get to know God better, we will find that He can be trusted in *all* things, even in those difficult times (*John 14:1+27*). He has a way of turning even bad things into something good, in the end, as we pray and look to Him (*Rom 8:26-28*).

God is for us not against us! (*Rom 8:31*). As we take anything that is hurting our hearts, honestly and openly to Him, [without fear of condemnation (*Rom 8:1*)] our hearts will begin to soften before Him and our communication with Him will enjoy the freedom. He already sees them, so we can't hide anything from Him anyway, but God is longing to 'chat', and to comfort and guide our hearts (*2 Cor 1:3-4*).

We have a promise from God, in 1 Peter 3:12+18, that 'the eyes of the Lord are on the righteous and His ears are attentive to their prayer…For Christ died for sins once for all, the righteous for the unrighteous, to bring you to God'. Of course we are not righteous by our own efforts, but we trust in the righteousness of Christ and everything He has done on our behalf (*2 Cor 5:21*). This gives us unlimited access to God! (*Eph 2:18-22*)

Paul writes in his letter to the Ephesians to pray continuously (*Eph 6:18*), because prayer is an attitude of heart more than words, but words express our hearts so they can be useful! It can be good to set aside a time committed to praying and have some time for just you and your God chatting to each other *(Mark 6:31 / Phil 4:6-7*). But it is also good to get together with a friend or with others to pray too (*Matt 18:19-20*)

Praying with others can be a very rewarding experience, as you share together and pray for each other's needs, and for other people you know. I once heard a child's prayer, which was: '*Dear God, sometimes I think about you, even when I'm not praying*'. That's a profound truth! God is with us all the time, so you and I are free to chat to Him anytime, anywhere, alone and with others (*Matt 28:18-20*)

One of the things I have sometimes used to help me pray is The Psalms, where I have taken the pattern of some words from one of the Psalms and put them into my own words to express my personal love and thanks to God. For example, *Psalm 139, verses 1-10*, can become a prayer from your heart to God's heart by speaking it out as used in the prayer below. The most important thing is that you enjoy spending time with your heavenly Father, and remember that He enjoys spending time with you!

Prayer
Dear Father, Thank You that you know all about me and still love me!
You know my thoughts and see everything that happens to me, for You are always
there. Thank You for placing Your hand of blessing upon my head. You are great
and too wonderful for me to ever fully understand, but I know that You promise
to remain with me for all eternity. For You are My strength and
support always, as You guide me every day. Amen

More articles, 'Teaching Letters' and 'Bible Studies' are available to view and download
on our website and also at: www.facebook.com/groups/gardenlandministries
If you would like to receive these by e-mail, please contact: gardenlandministries@gmail.com

Joshua 1:9 says that God will be with you wherever you go

MONDAY		Date
TUESDAY		Date
WEDNESDAY		Date
THURSDAY		Date
FRIDAY		Date
SATURDAY		Date
SUNDAY		Date

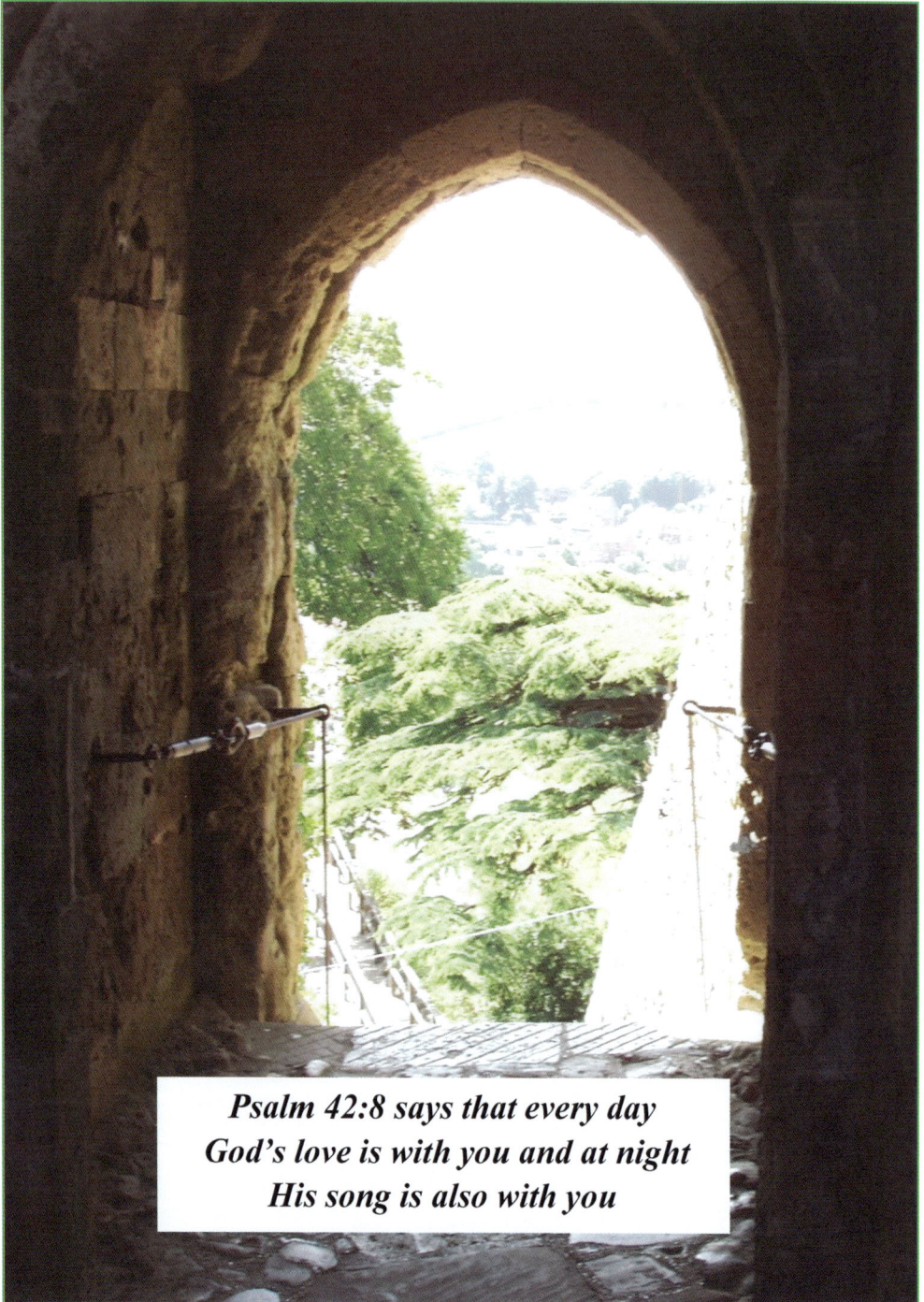

Psalm 42:8 says that every day God's love is with you and at night His song is also with you

MONDAY		
TUESDAY		
WEDNESDAY		
THURSDAY		
FRIDAY		
SATURDAY		
SUNDAY		

Jeremiah 29:11 says that
God has good plans for you

MONDAY		
TUESDAY		
WEDNESDAY		
THURSDAY		
FRIDAY		
SATURDAY		
SUNDAY		

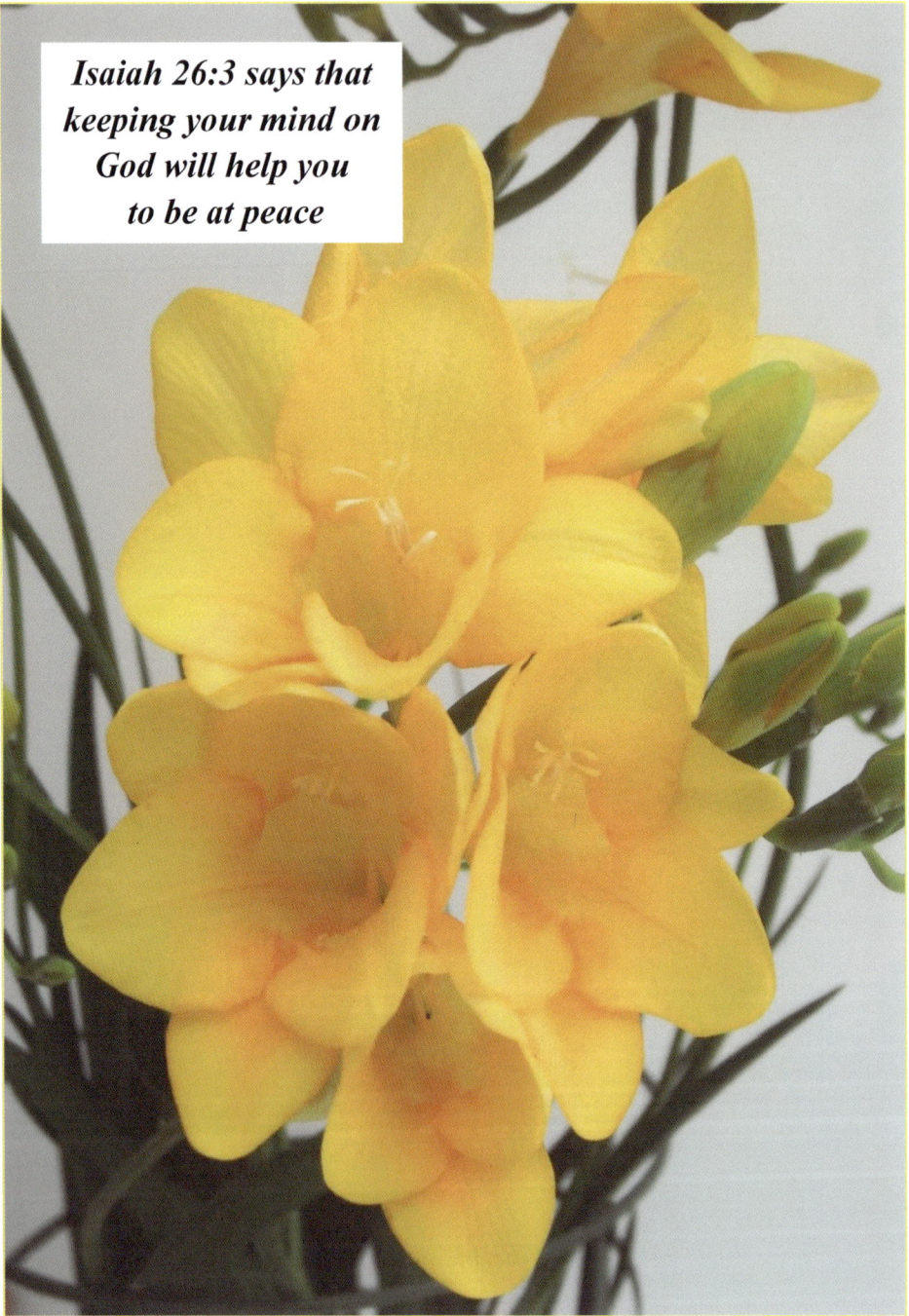

Isaiah 26:3 says that keeping your mind on God will help you to be at peace

MONDAY		
TUESDAY		
WEDNESDAY		
THURSDAY		
FRIDAY		
SATURDAY		
SUNDAY		

John 3:16-17 says that God loved you so much that He sent His Son to save you, not to condemn you

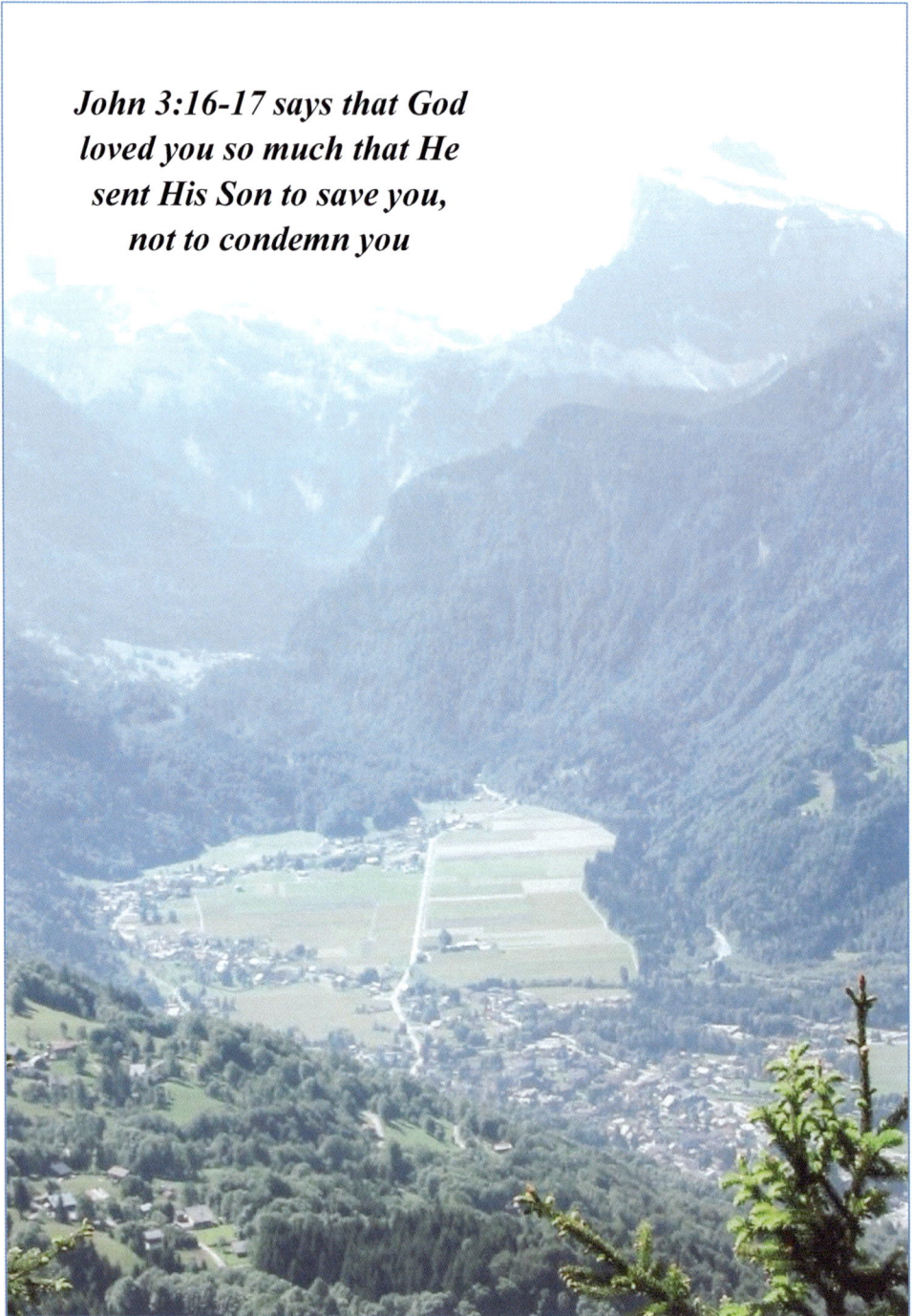

MONDAY		
TUESDAY		
WEDNESDAY		
THURSDAY		
FRIDAY		
SATURDAY		
SUNDAY		

Zephaniah 3:17 says that The Lord rejoices over you!

MONDAY		Date
TUESDAY		Date
WEDNESDAY		Date
THURSDAY		Date
FRIDAY		Date
SATURDAY		Date
SUNDAY		Date

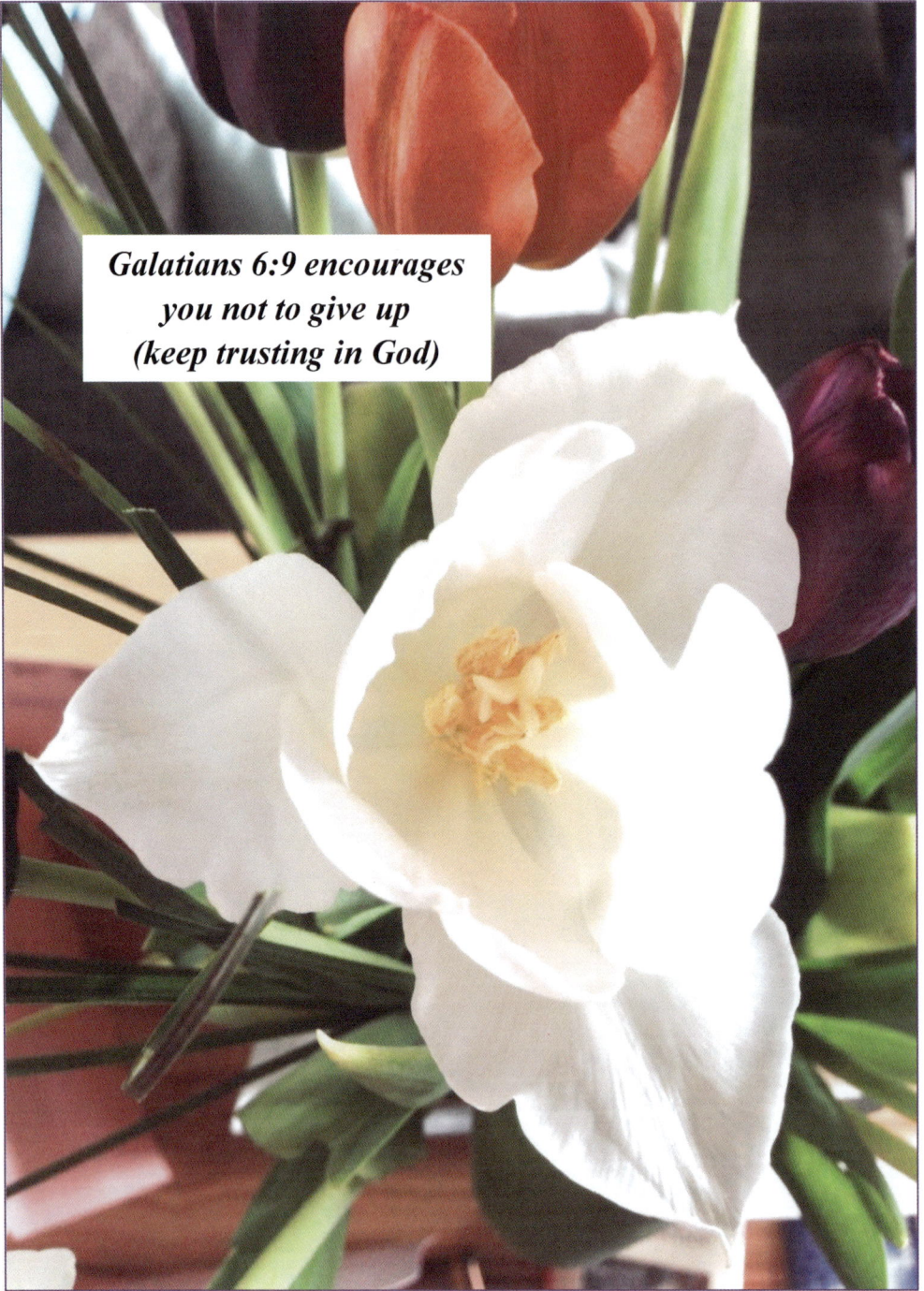

Galatians 6:9 encourages
you not to give up
(keep trusting in God)

MONDAY		Date
TUESDAY		Date
WEDNESDAY		Date
THURSDAY		Date
FRIDAY		Date
SATURDAY		Date
SUNDAY		Date

In Matthew 11:28 Jesus said to come to
Him for restoration when you are weary

MONDAY		
TUESDAY		
WEDNESDAY		
THURSDAY		
FRIDAY		
SATURDAY		
SUNDAY		

The praise and worship of God honours and glorifies Him *(Ps 50:23)* and The Bible tells us that God inhabits the praises of His people (*Ps 22:3*). There are also numerous benefits for the believer. Here are just a few examples:

Praising God......
1. brings joy and strength (***Neh 8:10)***
2. silences the enemy (***Ps 8:2***)
3. dispels spiritual darkness *(**Ps 27:1**)*
4. overcomes fear (***Ps 34:4-5)***
5. breaks through depression *(**Ps 34:6-7)***
6. releases healing (***Ps 103:1-3***)
7. brings deliverance (***Ps 71:23***)
8. builds faith (***Jude 1:20***)
9. calls 'things into being that are not as though they were' (***Rom 4:17)***
10. takes our minds off our problems and puts them back onto to God ~ who has and is the solution (***Heb 12:2-3)***
11. opens our hearts to listen to Him *(**Ps 42:8)***
12. gives peace to our souls *(**Ps 62:1-2)***

As you and I worship and praise Jesus, we are declaring all that He is and all that He has done (***Heb 13:15 / John 4:23-24***). It's amazing how proclaiming Jesus as Lord is actually good for us! (***Rom 10:9-10 / John 10:10***). When we do so, we are purposely putting Him as the center of our lives which releases His power to be at work in us and through us more effectively (***Phil 2:13 / Eph 3:20-21***).

It's good to remember too that *Isaiah 53:5* prophesied that Jesus would die for our sins and that He would also bring healing to us. When He was on earth, He certainly fulfilled His mission by healing all who came to Him (***Matt 8:16-17/ Matt 12:13-15***). At The Cross Jesus completed His work to bring both salvation and healing into the reach of all mankind (***Rom 5:8-10 / 1 Peter 2:24***).

The early church expected to see and experience healing as the Good News about salvation through Christ was shared with people. It seemed almost 'natural' for believers to expect to be in health (***3 John 1:2***).

As His Body here on earth, today (*1 Cor 3:16*), it is natural that we too have a heart to see people healed and whole, including ourselves. God has given His people the gift of The Holy Spirit, who Himself imparts spiritual gifts of healings to The Body of Christ (*1 Cor 12:9 / Acts 19:11-12*).

Scripture tells us that when believers lay hands on the sick, they would recover (*Mark 16:18b*) and when we pray for one oneanother in faith, we can expect to see healing follow (*Mark 2:3-5 / James 5:14-16*). Sometimes healing may take forms we don't understand or is progressive; however, it is still healing.

We need to trust God rather than depend on our own understanding (*Prov 3:5*). Jesus said that there would be times when we need to speak to our 'mountain' (*Mark 11:23*) to see the results we desire, and agreeing in prayer is powerful *(Matt 18:19-20)*.

God's will is to heal (*Matt 8:1-3*) and we need know this truth in our hearts (*Mark 11:24*). All healing is to the honour of Jesus, for it is His Name that is the most powerful in the universe (*John 14:13-14 / Acts 3:1-8*). It was through Jesus that God created everything that exists (*Col 1:16*). And God has placed a natural healing process within our bodies, which responds to physical resources too.

Although we are spiritual beings deep within our hearts, we still have physical bodies that live in a physical environment (*Gen 2:7 / 1 Cor 6:19*). Therefore, it is common sense to recognise that diet and environment can affect our physical health in a positive or negative manner.

Medicine, although made by man, can only be made using God's provision of ingredients (*John 1:3*); therefore appropriate use of helpful medicine can be productive to aid physical healing. But our final dependency needs to be on God Himself, for He is our ultimate source and provider of all good things (*Jer 29:11*).

Prayer:
Thank You Lord for all the different ways You help me. I pray that my soul
prospers and that I am in health as I consider Your Word above all else.
Thank You for all You have done and that You will complete the
good work You have begun in me! All to Your honour. Amen.

More articles, 'Teaching Letters' and 'Bible Studies' are available to view and download
on our website and also at: www.facebook.com/groups/gardenlandministries
If you would like to receive these by e-mail, please contact: gardenlandministries@gmail.com

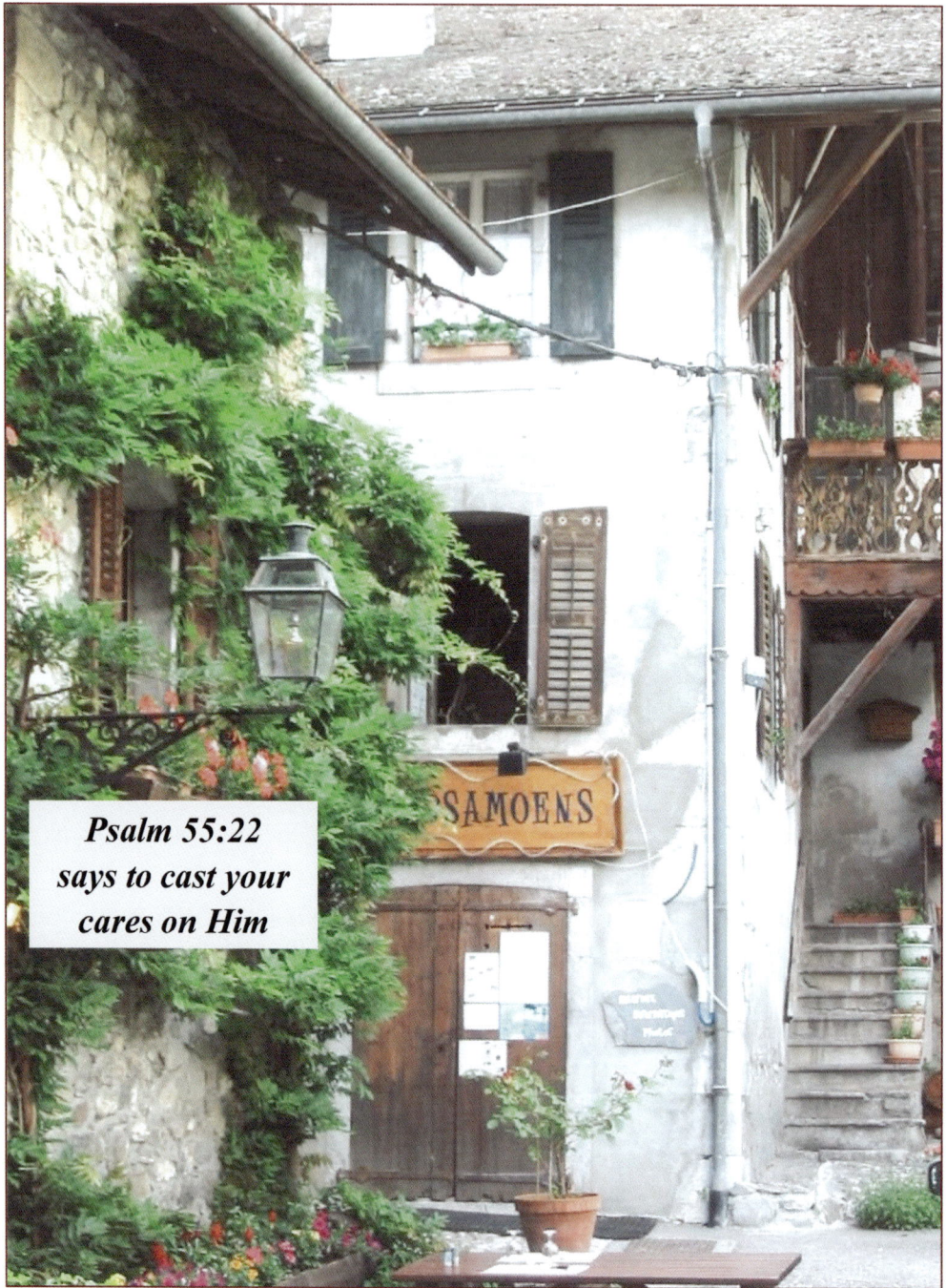

Psalm 55:22
says to cast your
cares on Him

MONDAY		
TUESDAY		
WEDNESDAY		
THURSDAY		
FRIDAY		
SATURDAY		
SUNDAY		

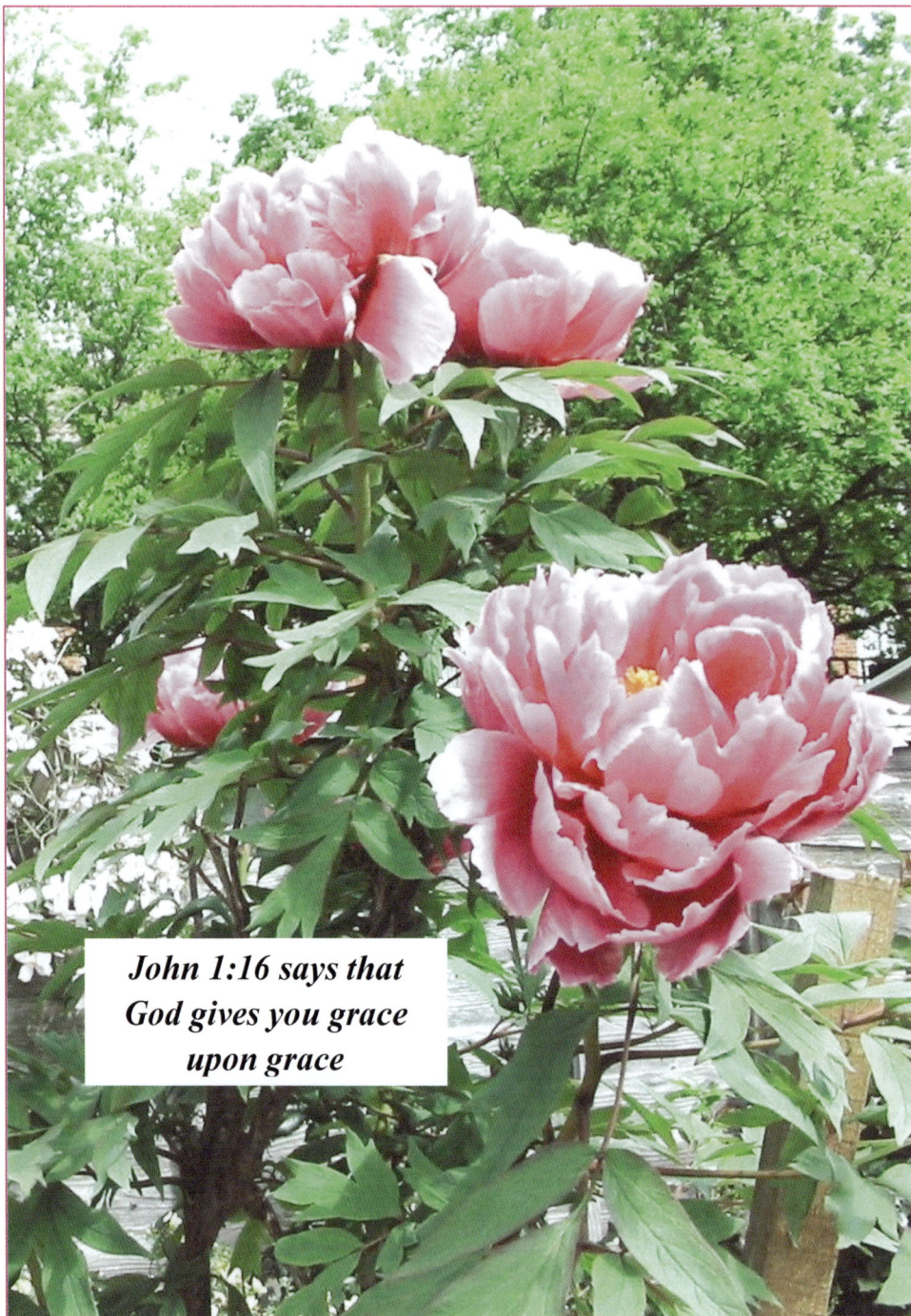

John 1:16 says that
God gives you grace
upon grace

MONDAY		Date
TUESDAY		Date
WEDNESDAY		Date
THURSDAY		Date
FRIDAY		Date
SATURDAY		Date
SUNDAY		Date

Psalm 4:8 says that God will help you to rest secure and be at peace

MONDAY		
TUESDAY		
WEDNESDAY		
THURSDAY		
FRIDAY		
SATURDAY		
SUNDAY		

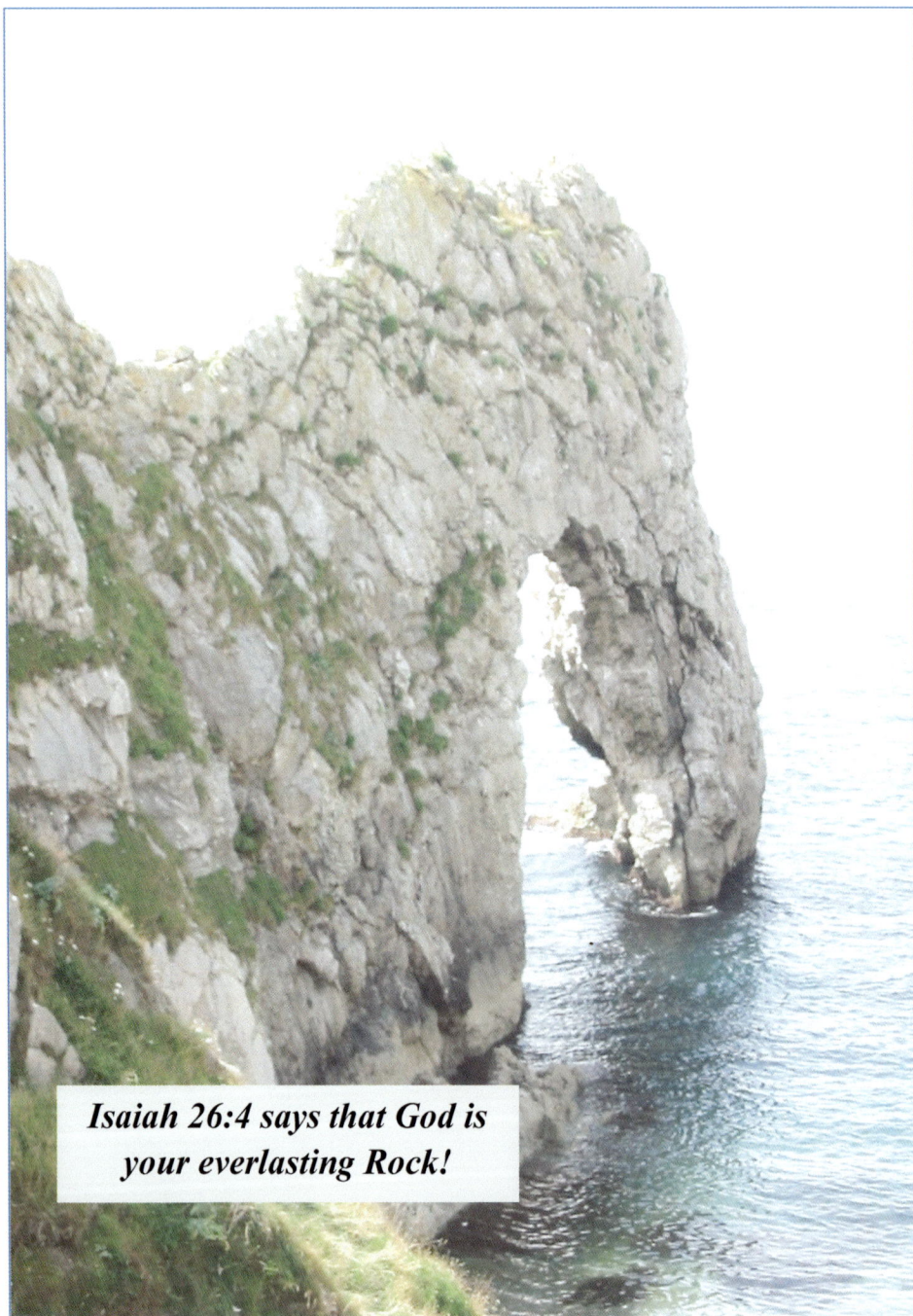

Isaiah 26:4 says that God is your everlasting Rock!

MONDAY		Date
TUESDAY		Date
WEDNESDAY		Date
THURSDAY		Date
FRIDAY		Date
SATURDAY		Date
SUNDAY		Date

Isaiah 40:8 says that God's Word will stand forever

MONDAY		
TUESDAY		
WEDNESDAY		
THURSDAY		
FRIDAY		
SATURDAY		
SUNDAY		

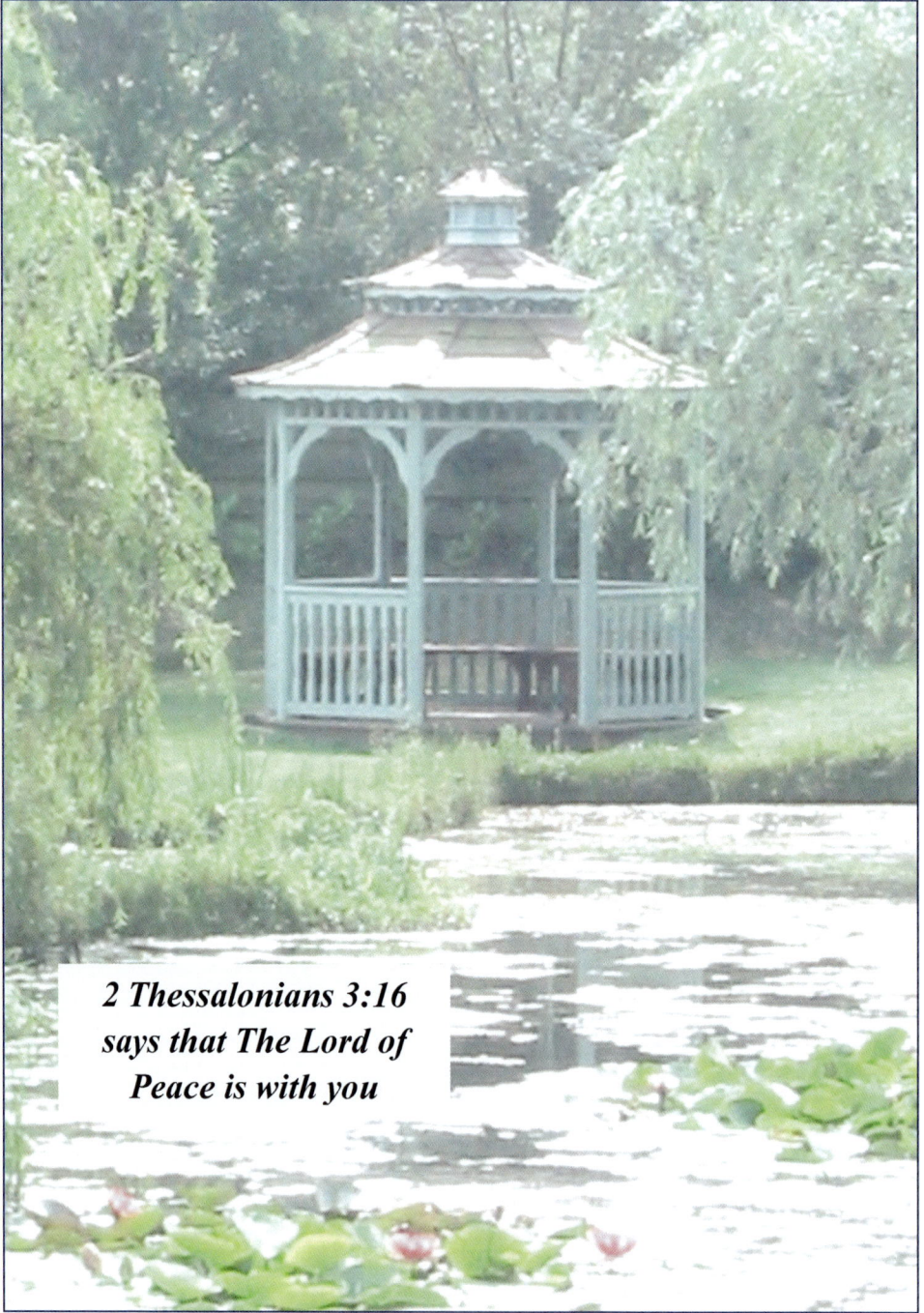

*2 Thessalonians 3:16
says that The Lord of
Peace is with you*

MONDAY		
TUESDAY		
WEDNESDAY		
THURSDAY		
FRIDAY		
SATURDAY		
SUNDAY		

Psalm 104:27 says that all creatures look to God

MONDAY		Date
TUESDAY		Date
WEDNESDAY		Date
THURSDAY		Date
FRIDAY		Date
SATURDAY		Date
SUNDAY		Date

Ephesians 2:8 says that by His love and His grace, God saves you

MONDAY		
TUESDAY		
WEDNESDAY		
THURSDAY		
FRIDAY		
SATURDAY		
SUNDAY		

*John 6:47 says that Jesus gives eternal
life to anyone who believes in Him*

MONDAY		
TUESDAY		
WEDNESDAY		
THURSDAY		
FRIDAY		
SATURDAY		
SUNDAY		

The Bible clearly tells us that Jesus has given us new freedom and that God does not condemn us through all Jesus has done for us (*Rom 8:1-2*). So why do we sometimes feel like we are still in bondage to our old life? One possibility can be that we experience a longing to cling to some of our 'old ways' because they are familiar and bring a sense of 'comfort' or 'stability' to our emotions when things are constantly changing around us. However, it is false comfort and false stability that provides a temporary fix to hurting emotions, but can never provide any real power or freedom to overcome a situation.

Mankind has been given free will by God, from the beginning of creation (*Gen 1:26-28*). Therefore we can make free choices in life, but those choices will and do affect you and I, and those around us. One of the many blessings of being 'free in Christ' is that Jesus has paid for all our sin for all time, therefore we do not need to come under guilt when we 'get things wrong' (*Rom 8:1*). However, it is an act of wisdom to use our wonderful freedom correctly through making right choices (*Prov 19:21 / Col 3:17*).

Jesus lives within every believer and just as He gave us His righteousness as a free gift, He also gave us freedom in Him (*Col 1:27 / Rom 5:17 / John 8:36*). For in Christ we have been 'reborn' into a new life which is strengthened as we set our thoughts on Him (*Col 3:1-2*). However, if we concentrate our thinking on past hurts and bondages, it becomes like carrying a heavy weight around that is not really there anymore. <u>Your new life is the reality</u> (*Matt 11:28 / Rom 6:4*).

When we receive Christ, we receive God's Holy Spirit who fills our lives with His power, and God becomes our Father (*Rom 8:14-16*). As His children, we are dearly loved and highly valued (*1 John 3:1*) for there is no favoritism from God (*Gal 2:6*).

God is at work IN you and I, and He is at work THROUGH you and I, because the new life we have been given is filled with the life of Jesus Himself (*Gal 2:20*)! Because of Him, every curse in your life is broken by all Christ has done (*Gal 3:13*) and God credits those who have faith in Him as righteous (*Gal 3:6*). This is good news!

God loves to speak to you and I personally (***John 10:27***) but the main source God will use to speak to us is through His Word (***2 Tim 3:16-17***). However, He will not contradict His Word, so this gives us security when discerning what we 'hear'; God is good and will only seek to do you good (***Jer 29:11***).

God has freely given us the blessings of Abraham, through Jesus (***Gal 3:16+26-29***), so with all this blessing, it is better to look to God for our approval rather than people (***Gal 1:10***) for we have been called by His grace and The Holy Spirit will gladly guide us into all truth (***John 16:13***). According to The Bible, keeping our thoughts on the goodness of God is the most reliable way to keep our hearts at peace (***Is 26:3***)

We experience our freedom in Christ at its best when we demonstrate what He has done for us though acts of kindness and maintaining loving fellowship with oneanother (***Gal 5:13-15***). The Holy Spirit has empowered us with the fruit of God's love, which is greater than our 'own' (***Gal 5:22-23***), and He has placed that great love deep within our hearts as believers (***Rom 5:5***). The result of living this way is that Jesus can be revealed to the world through His people as He really is, God of love (***John 13:35 / 1 John 4:8***)

What a privilege, what an honour! What a God of mercy, goodness and grace, that should desire to dwell in you and I (***1 Cor 3:16***). We can grow and experience the joy of this new life (***Rom 6:4***) and what it means for us by considering and applying the truth of God's Word to our everyday lives. We may sometimes feel like we are growing little by little and step by step, but we will grow stronger as we freely live in Him! (***Col 2:6-8 / Luke 17:21***)

Prayer:
Thank You Jesus for my living freedom! I am free to know God as He really is
and free to be the person You created me to be! I never have to perform for You!
I am loved and accepted already as His child, Your friend! I can cast all my cares on
You ~ I can overcome all those things that once held me back. The life I now live is
filled with Your life and purpose, Your goodness and love, which I embrace with
all of my heart, and give all the glory to You. Amen.

More articles, 'Teaching Letters' and 'Bible Studies' are available to view and download
on our website and also at: www.facebook.com/groups/gardenlandministries
If you would like to receive these by e-mail, please contact: gardenlandministries@gmail.com

Psalm 16:11 says that God makes His path of life known to you, to fill you with joy

MONDAY		
TUESDAY		
WEDNESDAY		
THURSDAY		
FRIDAY		
SATURDAY		
SUNDAY		

John 14:23 says that God makes His home in your heart through Jesus

MONDAY		
TUESDAY		
WEDNESDAY		
THURSDAY		
FRIDAY		
SATURDAY		
SUNDAY		

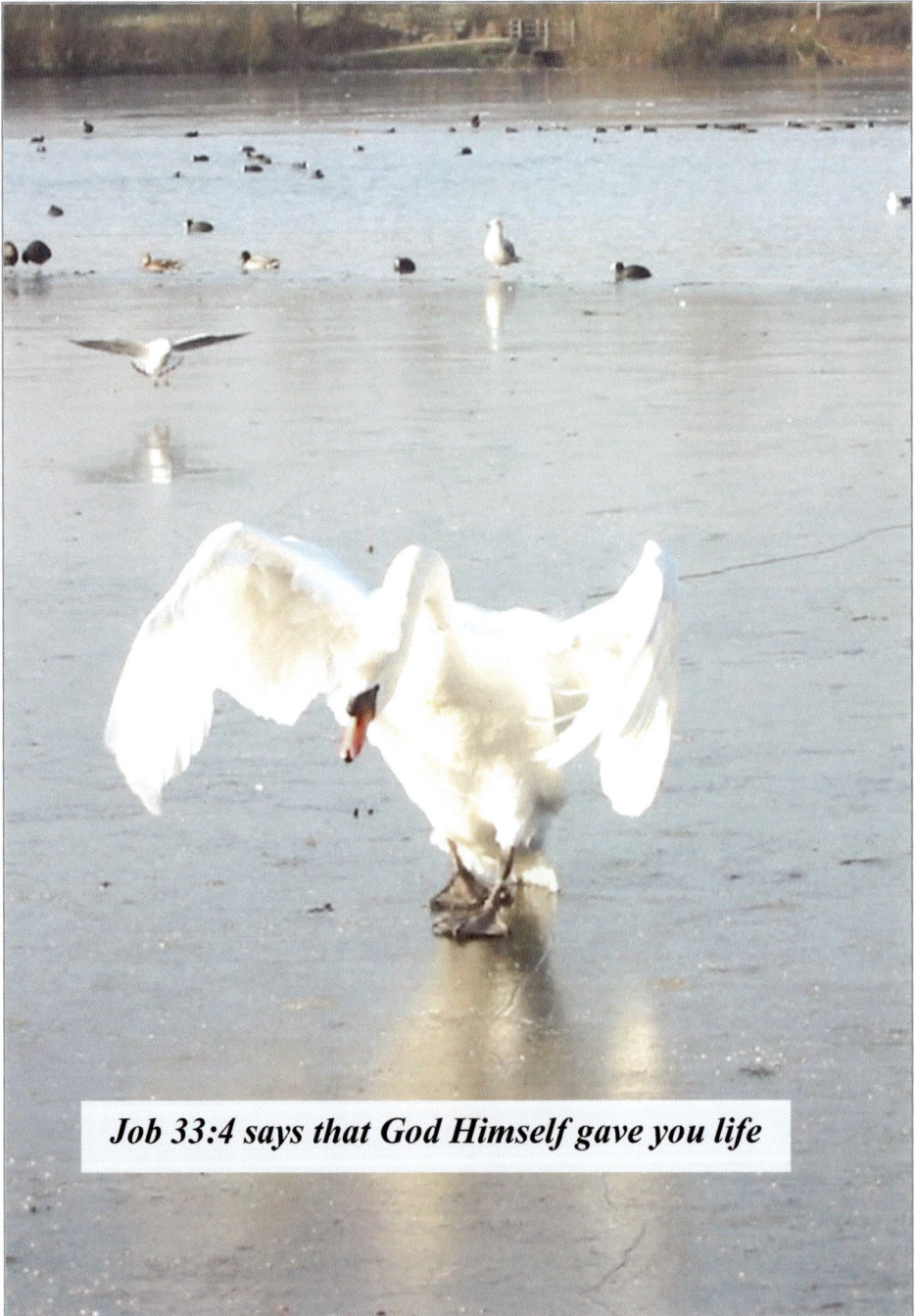

Job 33:4 says that God Himself gave you life

MONDAY		Date
TUESDAY		Date
WEDNESDAY		Date
THURSDAY		Date
FRIDAY		Date
SATURDAY		Date
SUNDAY		Date

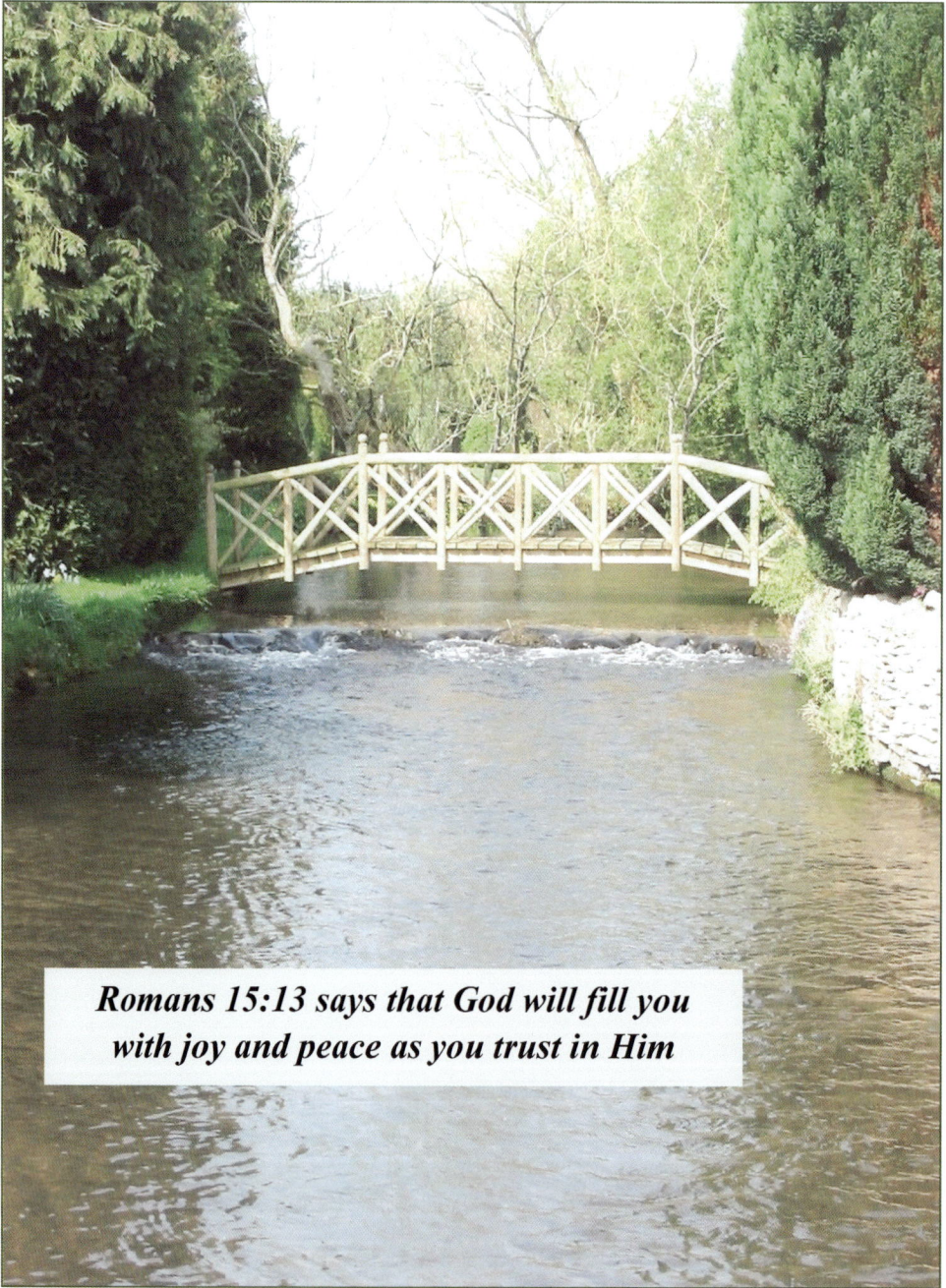

Romans 15:13 says that God will fill you with joy and peace as you trust in Him

MONDAY		
TUESDAY		
WEDNESDAY		
THURSDAY		
FRIDAY		
SATURDAY		
SUNDAY		

Deuteronomy 33:27 says that
God's everlasting arms support you

MONDAY		
TUESDAY		
WEDNESDAY		
THURSDAY		
FRIDAY		
SATURDAY		
SUNDAY		

Isaiah 54:10 says that even if the mountains were shaken, His love for you can never be shaken

MONDAY		
TUESDAY		
WEDNESDAY		
THURSDAY		
FRIDAY		
SATURDAY		
SUNDAY		

Romans 5:5 says that God has poured out His love into your heart

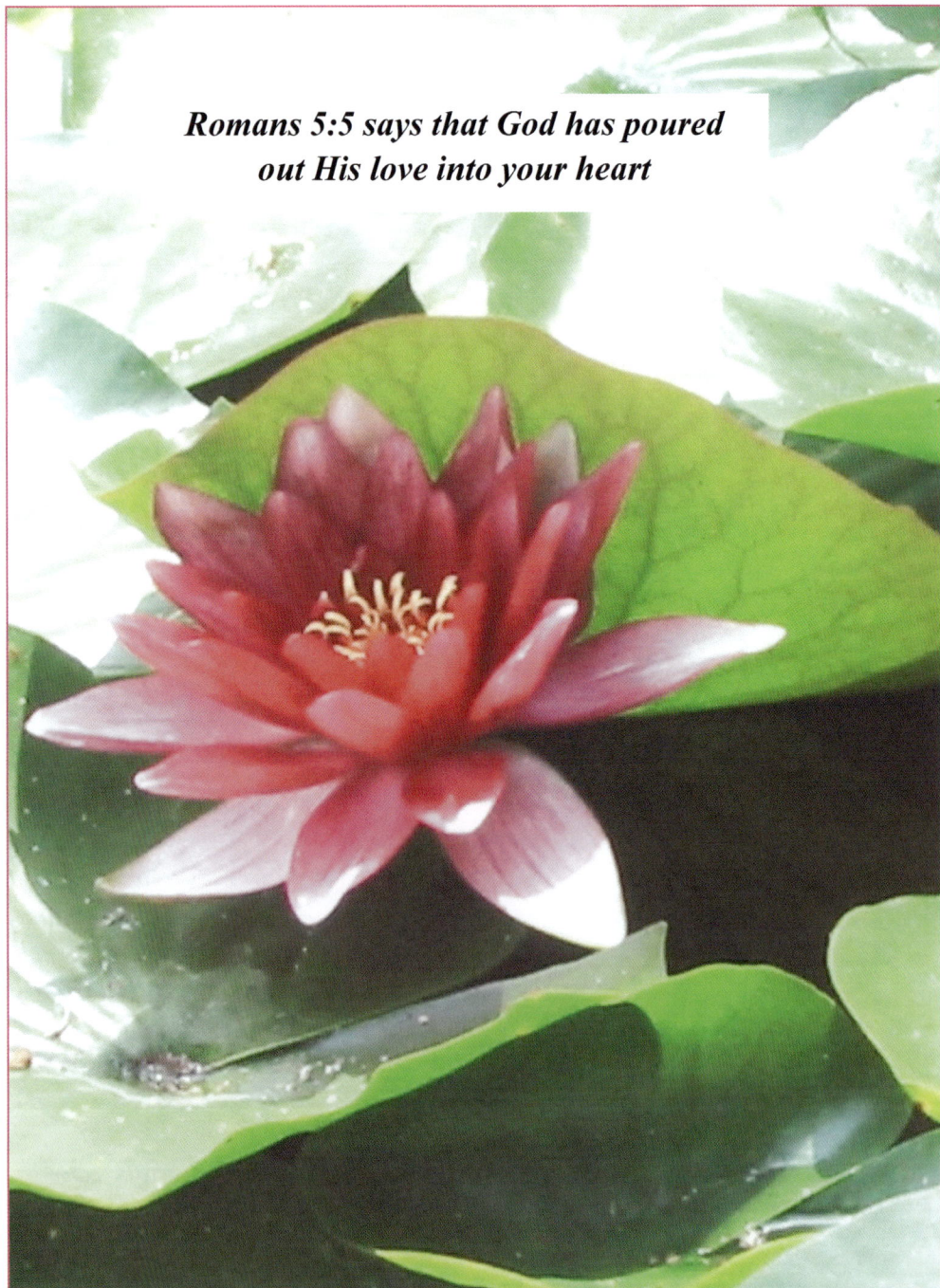

MONDAY		
TUESDAY		
WEDNESDAY		
THURSDAY		
FRIDAY		
SATURDAY		
SUNDAY		

Dairy Notes

Dairy Notes

Diary Notes

Diary Notes

Diary Notes

Diary Notes

May you always feel loved and protected

May you never lose sight of The Way

May you carry The Lord within your heart

And rejoice in Him every day

ABOUT THE AUTHOR AND GARDENLAND MINISTRIES

Carmel shares powerful insights throughout her books. She began by using her own testimony in her initial publication, then further books developed as her family and friends felt The Holy Spirit's lead for her to write more and more!

'Gardenland Ministries' developed over a period of time, after Christian friends and family gathered together with John and Carmel to learn more from God's Word using The Charis Bible College Correspondence Course.

God had laid many promises on the hearts of John and Carmel over the years, one of which is the Bible verse *Isaiah 58:11*, where God promises to guide always, restore and make people who trust in Him 'like a well-watered garden'.

The fellowship encouraged John and Carmel in their ministry, and from standing on the promise of Isaiah 58:11 the vision of Gardenland grew (more is shared about this in Carmel's first book: God's Fruitful Garden)

Gardenland's vision is to share the 'Good News' of Jesus: to declare that God came down as one of us, to live as one of us, and show Gods' heart of love and grace towards us.... as revealed through His Son *(Hebrews 1:1-3)*.

This is currently being fulfilled in John and Carmel's lives through writing easy to read books and offering free to download resources on their website at *www.gardenlandministries.org* as well as having various social media where posts of hope and encouragement are offered.

FACEBOOK PAGE (1): https://www.facebook.com/GardenlandBooks

FACEBOOK PAGE (2): https://www.facebook.com/Carmel-Carberry-Author

AUTHORS BLOG: https://carmelcarberry.wordpress.com/

TWITTER: https://twitter.com/CarmelCarberry

> # God is not counting your sins,
> # He is counting the hairs on your head!
> ## (2 Cor 5:19 / Luke 12:7)

HOPE AND ENCOURAGEMENT

PUBLISH His glorious deeds among the nations! Tell everyone about the amazing things God does!

Psalm 96:3

GOOD NEWS!

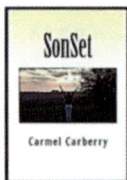
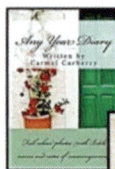

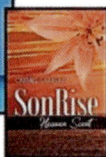

Gardenland Books (GLB)
Written by Carmel Carberry
https://carmelcarberry.wordpress.com

All the above books are available in paperback and kindle at Amazon across the world ~ easy reading! Please search for author 'Carmel Carberry' in the books department ~ simply sharing about Jesus, God's Son

God loved the world so much that He gave His One and only Son whoever BELIEVES in Him has ETERNAL LIFE

John 3:16

Printed in Poland
by Amazon Fulfillment
Poland Sp. z o.o., Wrocław